D0331478

Changing Places

Changing Places

A Journey with My Parents into Their Old Age

JUDY KRAMER

RIVERHEAD BOOKS
A MEMBER OF PENGUIN PUTNAM INC.
NEW YORK
2000

RIVERHEAD BOOKS
a member of
Penguin Putnam Inc.
375 Hudson Street
New York, NY 10014

Published simultaneously in Canada

Library of Congress Cataloging-in-Publication Data

Kramer, Judy.
Changing places : a journey with my parents into their old age /
Judy Kramer.
p. cm.
ISBN 1-57322-163-5
1. Aging parents—Care. 2. Parent and adult child. I. Title.
HQ1063.6.K73 2000 00-038708
306.874'3—dc21

Printed in the United States of America

1 3 5 7 9 10 8 6 4 2

This book is printed on acid-free paper. ∞

BOOK DESIGN BY DEBORAH KERNER

Acknowledgments

There are many people I want to thank for their help in bringing about the publication of this book. For their generosity in sharing this journey, for their review of much of the text before they died, and for the courage they modeled in facing the end of their lives, I am grateful to my parents, Milton and Evelyn Lieberman. I am deeply appreciative of my brother Dennis for his companionship on this journey and for his sharing in the decisions about our parents. For the time, compassion, and clarity she brought to commenting on the first draft of this book, I thank my friend Janet Lottero. For the years she spent helping me prepare for this journey, and the clear thinking and love she brought to the task of reading my manuscript and suggesting ways to improve it, I thank Jane McCauley, caring therapist and good friend. I thank my editors at the *Gazette* newspapers, Linda VanGrack Snyder, Ellyn Wexler, and Karen Shafer, who gave me a voice to share the journey. A special thanks to Helen Servator, my mother's best friend, and her daughter Sandi Ezrin, my best friend, for sharing these intimate moments in my life. Gratitude to my mentor, author Frank Strunk, who agreed to guide a total stranger through the shoals of writing a book. And to Hill Slowinski, whose advice was and continues to be greatly appreciated. To Harvey Wertlieb, who encouraged me, and Anne Messitte, who shared publishing experience, thank you. I want to thank my high school friends Maida Crocicchia and Renie Knudson for the long lunches we shared, the losses we talked about, and the comfort they gave.

I need to thank my agent Ned Leavitt for recognizing that the purpose of this book was not to tell someone how to help aging parents, but to explain what it felt like to do that. His understanding of that intent made publication possible. Deep thanks to my editor, Wendy Carlton, at Riverhead Books, for her sensitive suggestions, steadfast enthusiasm, and wise counsel. If the book gleams, it is because she polished it.

Much love and thanks to my children Andy, Paul, and Amy—for believing in the book, for encouraging me to write it, for cheering me on when it was hard and I was tired, and for sharing loving insights about their grandparents with me. There are no words adequate to thank my husband, Oscar, for helping me help my parents, for listening to each chapter, for sharing with me the passion to record this journey, and for providing the technical ability to print this manuscript. Engineer, companion, friend, thank you.

And finally I wish to thank the readers of the newspaper columns that gave rise to this book. When I was frightened by my journey, their letters and phone calls sustained me. When I was lonely, they comforted me. When I was exhausted, they energized and encouraged me. When I was sad they joined me. We are fellow travelers.

This book is dedicated
to my parents, Milton and Evelyn Lieberman,
whose journey this is;
to Jane McCauley,
who helped me understand where we were going;
to my husband, Oscar,
who helped me tell the story;
and to my children, Andy, Paul, and Amy,
who encouraged me and one day
will make their own journey with me.

Contents

PART V • *Morning* • SURVIVAL *199*

Each time of life
has its own kind of love.

—LEO TOLSTOY

Preface

This book is a travelogue of sorts, a record of my journey with my parents into their old age. It is the story of how our lives and love changed as we faced death together. And although the narrative deals with the deaths of my parents, this book is about living.

The text is chronological rather than thematic because life does not happen in neatly organized chapters. In this journey, events and emotions were often unexpected, things were sometimes chaotic. That is the nature of the experience.

Now, four years after beginning to write and two years after my parents' deaths, I can look back and see the long day's journey we made with each other. The story begins in the afternoon of my parents' lives, when their bodies have begun to fail them. It continues into the evening of their declining health and through the night of their deaths. It concludes with the dawn of my grief and finally the morning of my own survival. My parents and I were companions on a journey that none of us wanted to take. This is a book about what we discovered.

Changing Places

Introduction

They watched me be born and I watched them die, and the years in between bound us unbreakably. In the past four years, my parents and I have completed a fifty-six-year journey, traveling together into their old age—three very ordinary people caught in an extraordinary experience.

My father's health had declined slowly over a decade, finally resulting in end-stage renal disease requiring dialysis and skilled care in a nursing home. Three months later, when her diabetes made it impossible for her to continue to manage alone, my mother chose to join him. They moved into a safer environment and asked me to help them reorganize their lives.

There is nothing unique about this. It occurs daily around the world as parents age into infirmity, illness, and death, and their children are helpless to halt the process. But what I have found remarkable is the range of feelings I have had: I have loved my parents and hated them, been enraged with them and anguished for them, laughed with them and cried for them. I have prayed for their survival and wished for their deaths. And I wondered whether others felt as I did. Despite the comfort of family and friends, I have been very lonely.

Overwhelmed by my new responsibility for their lives, I began to record the impact of this experience on my own life in the form of a newspaper column that resulted in this book. It is not a "how-to" book and my parents and I are not experts. But we agreed to share our journey in the hope that it might prove helpful to others. The volume of letters and calls to the newspaper validated our decision. People wrote often to say they understood and felt connected, that we were telling *their* stories. Until they died, I read my parents each article before it was submitted. They were my first editors. It was their story as well as mine, and I wanted to get it right for all of us. They never changed a word, letting me tell the story as I felt it, as we lived it, and as it unfolded.

My mother, Evelyn Steinberg Lieberman, was born in 1913, the middle child and second daughter in a family of five. Her parents—immigrants from Poland—fled Eastern Europe to escape Jewish persecution, met in New York, married, and raised their children in Brooklyn. And my mother became part of a rich cultural broth, growing up in an Italian neighborhood and speaking only Yiddish until she entered grade school. Her father was a carpenter, a union man all his life—short, wiry, always worried about money and the future of his family. Her mother, a blue-eyed, brown-haired beauty, raised three children on the second floor of a two-story walk-up. In middle age, my grandmother went to school to learn to read and write in English so that she could stay in touch with my mother, who had moved to Washington, D.C., and become a government secretary.

My father, Milton Lieberman, also born in 1913, was the second child in a family of seven, the first son among three sisters and a brother. His father immigrated from Moscow at twenty-one to meet and marry the nineteen-year-old Chicago-born bride with whom he raised his family in Philadelphia, Pennsylvania, and Camden, New Jersey. My grandfather was a stocky young man with no trade or training. He became a jobber, selling dry goods to businesses. He eventually ended up in the shoe business with his entrepreneurial wife, selling shoes from the basement of their rented house. A young man during the depression, my father began his working life selling automotive supplies in New Jersey and attended university night school for several years before being moved by his company to Washington, D.C.

It was in Washington in 1938 that my parents met in a boarding house for young singles. They married within a year, and I was born in 1941. My mother became a full-time housewife, and to support his new family and the war effort, my father became a welder and returned briefly to Philadelphia to rivet gun turrets onto battleships. When the war ended, my brother was born, and my father moved to a new career as a grocer in partnership with a brother-in-law. After several years as store owners, they closed the business, and my father joined his parents and brother in the family shoe business. He owned several shoe stores with them and we moved often between Washington and New Jersey. In 1963 he sold his interest in the New Jersey store. He and my mother moved to Maryland to live near their married children.

Ordinary people. Ordinary lives. My mother spent her days at home, as prescribed by the times, raising her children, avidly reading novels, knitting and crocheting, and keeping the apartment spotless. In middle age she went to work as a bookstore cashier and worked for fifteen years. My father worked as a shoe salesman, listened to classical music, read broadly about modern art, and continued to add to his library of hundreds of books on history, religion, science, philosophy, and art. They put their children through college and saw them launched into careers and families of their own before retiring on social security and moving into an apartment subsidized for senior citizens. I am a solid product of the immigrant dream, a middle-class one-time English teacher who married an engineer and raised three children before finding my calling as a writer.

There is nothing remarkable about this story except the response to my telling it. Although parental loss is a universal experience, we rarely share our feelings about it with each other. I hope this book can begin to fill that enormously empty space in which we find ourselves as our parents age and die. For me, there has been great comfort in discovering companions.

PART I

Afternoon

Changes

In the afternoon of their lives my parents need my help. As their bodies gradually begin to shut down, I am asked to shop with them and then for them. I am asked to write their checks and then to manage their debts. I am asked to drive them to the doctors and then to control their health care. Finally, Mom and Dad find it necessary to give up their independent living and move out of their apartment into a nursing home. Because it is their bodies that are failing and not their minds, the decision to make this change is initiated by them and supported by my husband and me. My brother, who lives five hundred miles away, concurs, and it becomes our job to make it happen.

None of us realizes then that the move will change the nature of our relationships with each other profoundly and that we will find ourselves two years later, at the closure of their lives, with very different bonds of kinship.

Even though adults may have been independent for a long time, the afternoon love between parent and adult child often still carries some of the taste of childhood dependence. Parents still maintain the flavor of wisdom and experience, still pantomime the role of caretaker, still wield the power of approval and disapproval. As they age into frailty, their new dependence on their grown children throws all established patterns into chaos. Every previous role is up for renegotiation. And love must wend its way through a maze of new feelings that now may include strong doses of resentment and anger, mixed with pain and compassion. Often, the sadness over difficult aspects of our relationships gives way to enormous grief with the realization that there is no longer hope for improvement. Time has run out.

For me, along with changes in the balance of power, come changes in the nature of love. I find myself feeling protective of my parents in new and disquieting ways. Just as I was once under the cover of their umbrella, they now seek shelter under mine. I give up a love that depends upon my parents and assume a new kind of love that is responsible for their welfare.

1

"Why did you give away that book?"

DEPARTURE: CLOSING A HOME

My parents have asked me to accompany them on a most interesting trip. I'm fifty-two and they are both eighty. When I was a child we vacationed in New York and New Jersey. Beaches mostly. This trip is different. I'm doing the driving and although we know where we're going, we don't know the best way to get there. But whatever the route, we're traveling together. It is a journey into my parents' old age.

The trip began this year when both of my parents realized that although they were alert and mentally competent to manage their own lives, their bodies were beginning to send clear messages that periodic tune-ups would no longer keep the engines running. Blurring vision could not be corrected. Hearing could not be restored. Shaking hands could no longer write checks and dispense medicines. And the toll of end-stage renal disease, dialysis, and diabetes made it impossible for them to trust the strength of their legs. Walking was no longer a given.

In a painful and difficult joint decision, they, my brother, my husband, and I concurred that it was time for them to be living in a safer environment. They needed to be in a place where when they fell, fainted, or became ill, medical help would be close at hand. This winter, when they moved into a nursing home, we began a trip that has already been replete with poignant road stops and unexpected negotiations. So I have decided to write a travelogue of sorts, because I have a sense that we are not without fellow travelers.

It took me seven months to understand that for my parents, the difference between "taking away" and "letting go of" their possessions and their responsibilities depended upon involving them in the decisions.

In their tiny one-bedroom apartment, my father ferociously collected as much of the world as space would allow. His books, albums, clippings, videotapes, and piles of newspapers nurtured him in the isolation that often results from illness and aging. As his presence in the outside world diminished, he sought to bring more of the world into his very limited personal space. For my mother, the joy of life focused around being able to continue to crochet the dazzling afghans that have made her famous in our extended family.

When they moved to the nursing home, both of my parents selected a concentrated core of belongings to take with them as their personal space was reduced from a three-room apartment to the one room they would share. After several weeks settling into their new surroundings, my brother and I brought both of them back to their apartment for one last selection before we dismantled their home.

It was a difficult morning, both of them sitting in wheelchairs deciding whether to toss or keep an eighty-year-old collection of things attaching them to the world and to each other. And when it was over, my brother and I were left with the task of removing what remained. We took, donated, gave away, or threw out books, china, videotapes, files, furniture.

With all of this planning and the involvement of my parents in the decision-making process, I was unprepared for their reactions in the weeks that followed. "Where are all of my videotapes?" "I had that hammer for fifty years and I could really use it now. It had a lot of memories for me." "Did you save that painting? Who has it?" "Why did you give away that book?" Each question was painful to hear. Each request was an accusation that caused me to feel guilty, angry, and sad. "Did you tell me to save it?" I responded angrily. "I thought you would know," was their response. Silently, the battle lines were drawn. They were hurt and angry and so was I.

Finally the discomfort level became too high. I went to visit them and we talked about the need for them to let go of their possessions and live in the present. We talked about the difference between having something taken away and deciding to let it go. We talked about control, and the fact that they had made some difficult decisions, and so had I. We shared our mutual pain and mourned the losses. And slowly, they began to attach themselves to their new lives. Family photographs appeared along the windowsill. Newspapers and books lay about looking well used.

But as I left the nursing home that afternoon, I began to have a sense of the journey that lay ahead. I saw the road, but not the roadblocks. And I braced myself for the rest of the trip.

2

"The nursing home really needs me."

MOVING IN

Being needed is a vital and sustaining part of life. When my father moved into the nursing home, he said good-bye to many of his hundreds of long-treasured books and his enormous stuffed rocking chair. Driving to the nursing home, he shared with me his feelings about saying good-bye to his freedom as well. Neither of us dreamed that within half a year, the nursing home would become his reason for wanting to live.

The call came into my office late in the afternoon. "Dad's in the hospital. Please hurry." On my birthday, my father had stopped breathing. Staff at the nursing home, working frantically, had kept him alive with CPR. Paramedics in the ambulance revived him. Doctors and nurses in the emergency room slapped an external pacemaker on his chest and stabilized his heart. He was still with us. But this was a close one. It was time to speak once again about living wills and last wishes.

We had been through this before following heart surgery, kidney surgery, gall bladder surgery, brain surgery. We spoke quietly as the oxygen bubbled reassuringly in a bottle next to his bed. "Dad, if this happens again, go over with me what you want done," I said. And his answer stunned me. "Before I moved into the nursing home, I would have said, 'Let me go.' But now that I see how good it can be, I want to live." "What's good about the nursing home?" I asked.

"They really need me there," he told me. "When they found out that I love to write, they encouraged me to teach a class in creative writing. I have two students who are older than I am. They sometimes repeat themselves, but we share and they write and it's good. They have stories about their lives to tell." He thought for a few minutes and then continued. "When I complained about the food, they put me on a committee to evaluate food service and make suggestions. And then they asked me to read one of my essays in the talent show." Dad warmed to his story. "I offered to present a slide show about modern art and they were really excited about it."

As the high-tech monitors hummed in the background recording each heartbeat and confirming his return to life, my father described how the nursing home had really been built with its residents in mind. He expressed his joy at sitting next to the wall-to-wall windows and being able to look out onto the courtyard. He talked about the trees, the birds, the sunshine, and his pleasure at feeling connected to the natural world. He mentioned how much he appreciated having a shelf built in his room to house his favorite books. "The halls have windows at the end and are light. They feel wide and open. Mom and I have a table in the dining room next to the window and we can watch the world. We feel connected."

And he talked about how the administrators try to work out any friction between residents and staff. "Whenever Mom and I have complained about something involving the staff, the social worker or head of nursing will call a meeting so that we can all problem-solve together."

Hearing my father speak so eagerly about wanting to live, I realized the power of feeling needed instead of needy. My father's intellect is miraculously intact, but I have come to believe that for the frail elderly, regardless of their level of awareness, the opportunity to continue to contribute is a reason to continue to live.

3

"She was letting go of her money. I was taking over."

ASSUMING CONTROL

Control is changing hands. Many months before my mother entered the nursing home, I had opened the checkbook she had kept meticulously for fifty-four years and felt a tremendous sense of loss when I saw how her once beautiful handwriting had deteriorated into squiggly words and jagged numbers that I could barely read.

The effort she obviously had put into the last several months of bill paying touched me deeply and I respected her unflagging efforts to keep doing her job. My eyes met hers across the kitchen table and I sensed the frustration, rage, humiliation, and sadness she was feeling at yet another loss to the aging process.

"It's OK, Mom," I said with a bravado I did not feel. "Just tell me what to do and I'll do it." And with those words, I assumed responsibility for my parents' finances. It was like assuming the reins of a runaway stagecoach. The dollars hadn't gotten out of control. Mom always knows to the penny what she has and what she spends. But the paper work had engulfed her life and occupied most of the eating space at the small table. The magnifying glass that she painstakingly used to read the mail was at the top of the heap.

With trepidation I began to sort through the piles of envelopes: household bills, health insurance claim forms, doctors' bills, Medicare statements, hospital bills, banking statements, renewal forms, credit card statements. This was not an invasion of privacy. It was an invasion of identity. She was letting go of another bit of independence, and I was taking over.

At first we did it together. I would go over to my parents' apartment on the fifteenth and thirtieth of every month, read my mother the bills and statements, and write the checks. That lasted for about a year. Then this winter, when they moved into the nursing home, the stagecoach was all mine, and the ride has been exhausting. Some expenses disappeared (rent, utility bills, Meals on Wheels bills, household insurance bills, food bills) only to be replaced by the more consolidated and complex bills of the nursing home, pharmacy, and different Medicare coverage. Periodically I needed (and still need) to take time off from work to pay their bills and make the necessary phone calls, when totals don't add up or an expensive medication is listed for an ailment I don't know about.

When you pay someone else's bills, you become intimately connected to many of the private areas of their lives. Every rash, infection, long distance phone call, and personal hygiene product translates into an entry you have to pay for. Every visit to the mailbox is preceded by dread of the pile you will remove. I found that the only way I could manage this new role was to compartmentalize my mental and physical space. I designated a huge wicker basket for all of my parents' mail. I set aside an entire desk for their record-keeping. And I filled one shelf in my pantry with individual notebooks for their medical expenses, legal documents, nursing home costs and records, doctors' bills, and banking records. I worked at updating them whenever I had to and whenever I could fit it into my life.

There came a point at which my parents and I agreed that they no longer wanted to know all the details of their financial lives. I had the power of attorney for them, and seeing their savings diminish so quickly was only causing them worry and sadness.

And so we have arrived at a process that is difficult but working. They are trusting me and I am trying to keep up with the recurrent waves of responsibility. Because I often work into the evening, I cannot visit them as often as I would like. And I regret not being able to walk these last miles with them more personally. However, it gives me a sense of peace and even satisfaction that by driving the coach, I am giving them a more comfortable ride. But I still miss my mother's handwriting.

4

"Now that we've planned their funerals, what happens if they don't die?"

SETTING UP AN IRREVOCABLE TRUST

It was time to talk of funerals. My brother and I sat in a magnificently appointed windowless room. The deep carpet and the rich mahogany conference table that separated us seemed to call for reverential whispers and uncomfortable silences. We waited for the funeral director.

Our parents had not died. We had just left them busily going about their day at the nursing home. But caution, bankers, and lawyers had driven us to this place. Among the new terminologies we had learned was the phrase "irrevocable trust." We had been advised to set aside some of our parents' money in advance to cover their funeral expenses. That money would not be considered part of their estate and would remain in place until needed. Mom and Dad elected to have no part in this. They were too busy with the challenges of living to deal with the details of dying. They asked us to make the arrangements.

I, of course, had attended many funerals. But this was my first experience behind the walls of ritual we have established to make death bearable. This was business. My brother and I sat and listened to the air conditioner whistle. Like nervous children, we tried not to smile too much and were glad of each others' company.

The funeral director finally came in, a small round man, dark suit, muted tie, younger than I had expected. He spoke with both empathy and eagerness. We explained the purpose of our visit and quickly became enmeshed in the minutiae of death: prescribed religious rituals, transportation, refrigeration, preparation of remains, casket selection, cemetery preparation, monuments. Each item carried with it a nonnegotiable sticker price. We felt swept along by waves of religious, societal, and legal requirements.

The room full of caskets was not as frightening as I had imagined. And my brother has a wonderful gift for comic relief. As we wandered through the maze of selections, gasping internally at the costs, he kept up a low-key patter of jokes that helped relieve the tension. We agreed on a casket and returned to the conference room.

The irrevocable trust was drawn up, selections were noted, and costs were listed. Dying is more expensive and complicated than either of us had imagined. The trust, a legal document, was full of incomprehensible legalese. Rather than complete the document and sign it in ignorance, we decided to share it with our lawyer first. Once he translated it for us and assured us that we and the funeral home were meeting the requirements of the law, we returned to sign the trust and write the check. It was the largest check I had ever written and my hands shook as I signed it. I felt a special responsibility, since the money I was spending was not my own.

We left the funeral home and walked across the parking lot taking deep breaths to relax. Stopping at the car, my brother turned, and with only a hint of a grin on his face, he asked, “Now that we have planned their funerals and paid for them, what happens if they don’t die?” We laughed halfway home.

I thought about the irony of the name of the transaction we had just completed. It was called an irrevocable trust. And isn’t that, after all, the bond that links parents and their children?

5

"A sad journey into emptiness."

MEDICAID: BECOMING POOR AND ELIGIBLE

The money is running out. I have found something better than an alarm clock to wake me up before sunrise in these waning days of winter. It’s Medicaid, the government’s health assistance to the poor. I must show that my parents have become poor so that they will be found eligible. It’s a sad journey into emptiness.

Mom and Dad are knocking at the door of poverty, and I have led them to this place. After a lifetime of hard work, my parents had carefully accumulated a nest egg that they felt would carry them through their old age. But time has robbed the nest and my parents have outlived the resources of the egg.

Weeks ago, when I carried my huge gray plastic laundry basket full of heavy white notebooks into the elevator at the elder law attorney's office, I had no idea how I would help Mom and Dad pay for what remained of their lives. Inside the basket, lined up like sentinels, was my meticulous documentation of their past year's expenses: the nursing home book, the doctors book, the health care book, the banking book, and the legal book. The money had run out, and these notebooks were my map of their financial past and my guide to their future.

When I assumed responsibility for my parents' care and was authorized by them to act on their behalf, it was like opening a dark closet and having all my worst nightmares tumble out. The papers of their lives began to arrive at my house thick and fast: doctors' bills, subscription notices, bank statements, insurance reminders, hospital charges. I spent hours sorting, recording, phoning, paying, trying to balance the responsibility for their lives with the obligations of my own. Work at the office melded into work at home.

In the process of moving my parents into a nursing home, my brother and I had inadvertently thrown out many of their important papers. So for three months I found myself dragging the notebooks from one bank to another trying to reconstruct their lives and fill in missing documents.

I have spent hours on the phone calling insurance companies to find out the face value and cash surrender value of my father's insurance policies. I have visited banks to cash certificates of deposit, close accounts, and consolidate finances. I have hovered over my mailbox waiting to receive insurance documents that both of my parents must sign in order for me to account for all their assets. And all of this must be completed according to an exquisitely absolute time line. On the day that my parents apply for Medicaid, they must each have no more than $2,500 in assets . . . to the penny. I have to make this happen.

My husband and I have spent hours at the computer calculating their monthly expenses, tracking their bills, projecting how far their resources will carry them. With the help of an attorney, we have determined that my parents will be poor on May 1, 1994.

I have been told that I must have copies of their social security cards, birth certificates, all nursing home bills, three years of back bank statements, documentation of the funeral trust with current statement of value, notice of social security monthly benefits, copies of Medicare and health insurance cards, including a copy of the monthly health insurance premium statement, and letters stating insurance policy cash surrender values. And I must find this, get this, and do this in the hours before and after work.

This is what creeps into my consciousness as I drift in and out of sleep on these cold end-of-winter mornings. This is what makes me tremble as I lie in bed fighting fear and searching for the strength to get up. I've gotten most of it together . . . but not all of it. I have to begin making copies of everything so that I will have a notebook of record. I hold at bay all the what-ifs that crowd my mind and tell myself "just do it." Having guided my parents to this door, I find myself saddened and intimidated by the prospect of opening it. And when the door does open, I know myself well enough to understand that I will be replacing all my what-ifs, with what-nexts.

6

"I searched a long time for a sense of community."

CONFINEMENT, CONTENTMENT, AND COMMITMENT

Change was in the air. My father had dressed up for his graduation and I marveled as he walked toward me at how alive and engaged he looked. He was obviously proud of himself and I echoed his pride. He had completed his course of physical therapy and reached his goal of walking independently with a walker. The nursing home had called to invite me to the recognition ceremony and I was delighted to attend.

It seems that almost every time I visit my parents, I learn something new. At the age of eighty, they are still my teachers. Today, my father is teaching me about growing old, about having dreams and goals, and about community.

The living room was bustling with staff, residents, and family members. What surprised me most was how bubbly and excited the staff members were. The head of the physical therapy department wore a cap and gown. Graduation certificates lay rolled in a triangular pile, each tied with a white ribbon. Cameras whirred. Before the ceremony began, an announcement was made that each graduate would have his or her picture taken and could request a family photograph as well. The nursing home had stocked up on Polaroid film so the results could be shared immediately.

As wheelchairs were locked into place and residents were settled in their seats, the celebration began. My father introduced me to the elderly woman sitting beside me. Edna was a short, beautiful woman with rosy cheeks that matched her brightly flowered dress. Dad whispered that she was a delightful person, always very upbeat. Edna smiled and asked me if I had been at the Harvest Dance the previous night. She explained that she was sorry my dad hadn't made it, but she had had a good time. I thought again about the opportunities this nursing home was providing.

As each graduate's name was called, the mistress of ceremonies mentioned the goal that each had set and achieved. "Mr. Smith's goal was to be able to walk in the hallway independently and he can do that now. Mrs. Bryan's goal was to walk using a cane and only one person for support. She has achieved her goal." Each announcement was accompanied by a flurry of applause and a photograph. I looked carefully at each elderly face as recognition was conferred. Almost every one was alive with anticipation and pleasure.

My father quietly began to tell me about each resident being honored. "The woman with the dark streaked hair, she exercises every day and is religious about attending the maintenance classes. . . . The woman in the red shirt, she always encourages everyone. . . . The man without legs, he's really amazing, so positive. He walks with prosthetics and has the most wonderful attitude. He's an inspiration." And even before the word came to my mind, I felt the feeling of community.

After the ceremony and the pictures came the hot hors d'oeuvres, cookies, and punch, a social time during which my father introduced me to the resident who had helped save his life when he had gone into cardiac arrest. When Mary saw my father lose consciousness, she had immediately abandoned her walker and wheeled him to a nurse. Her quick response allowed the staff to begin CPR immediately and save him. I thanked her and sat back and listened to the two of them talk. "You know, Milton," she said to my father, leaning forward for emphasis, "I worry about you. When you try to walk with only a cane, you seem so unsteady. I know that this worries your wife. You must be more careful." Community unexpectedly popping up again.

I thought back to my parents' first few months at the nursing home. I had been so uncomfortable around the other residents. So many of them looked disengaged, vacant, unresponsive. The staff had also sometimes seemed distant. But slowly I began to see instances of caring and interconnectedness, moments between staff and residents, and among residents as well, that reflected friendship and respect. Of course, this was not always the case. But I saw enough to convince me that what can make a nursing home experience bearable, even positive, is a sense that other people care about you, that you are neither abandoned nor alone. And along with this realization came an increase in my own comfort level. I joined the community too.

As we walked back to his room, my father almost read my mind. "You know, " he began, "in my life, I searched a long time for a sense of community. Surprising that I should have found it here."

The next time I visited my parents, I passed Mary in the hallway. "Hello, Mary. How are you?" I asked. Mary smiled a full-faced smile. "You know me!" she responded with surprise. And that is what my father and this nursing home have taught me. Community is possible anywhere if you make and take advantage of the opportunity. People need to feel that they belong.

7

"What goes around comes around."

NURTURING CREATIVITY

The seasons are changing and so is Dad. My father waited all year to celebrate the coming of autumn. The window in his room is a wall-to-wall mural of enormous trees and my father has often talked with me about his pleasure at watching the seasons reflected in the branches. The first summer came and he loved it as the trees greened and blossomed. But he anticipated the fall with special relish. He had his camera ready months in advance.

And so one afternoon in late October, on the day before I began a new job that would make daytime visits rare, we went for a walk. It was the day we had both been waiting for: clear, bright, crisp, dappled with blazing gold and brilliant orange colors. The air smelled clean as I wheeled my father outside, and the breeze was soft. There was a small park with a tiny lake and a fountain about a mile down the road. I aimed in that direction and began to push.

My dad felt weighty in the chair, heavier than I had expected, and I worried that perhaps we had planned to go too far. The sidewalk was inclined slightly and I felt challenged by the exercise. As I huffed and puffed behind him, Dad was silently relaxed. When he spoke, it was to note a particularly beautiful tree or comment about his pleasure at being outdoors. I was grateful for the curb breaks and inclines that allowed us to cross streets so easily.

As I pushed my father along the bumpy sidewalk, the rhythmic sound of his wheels going over the cracks made me recall my own childhood pleasure at roller-skating down a hill and hearing the same regular beat, feeling the gritty vibrations of steel wheels on pavement. And I thought, "What goes around comes around." How many times, I wondered, had my father pushed my baby carriage up hills.

Dad interrupted my daydreaming when he asked me to stop. It was time to do what he had waited for . . . take some pictures. Since he had had a stroke some fifteen years earlier, holding a camera had become a real challenge. As I posed at his direction beneath a lemon yellow tree, I watched my father sitting in his wheelchair and juggling the camera into position. Twice it slipped out of his hand and was saved from destruction by the cord he had looped around his neck. Finally he had the camera in position, and as he clicked the shutter to preserve a picture of me, my mind's eye reciprocated in kind and captured an indelible image of his creative spirit still asserting itself.

We went to the lake, talked, sat and watched the leaves fall, took more pictures of each other. The walk back to the nursing home was fun because it was a long downhill roll. It wasn't until several weeks had passed, and my father had the photographs safely preserved in his album, that he shared his thoughts with me. "You know," he confided with a warm smile, "when we went for that walk I couldn't help remembering all of the times I had pushed you in your carriage and pulled you in your wagon." And the pictures he took are worth a thousand words.

8

"I couldn't eat the turkey rump."

PREPARING FOR MORTALITY

Mom and Dad are missing at the Thanksgiving table and things are not the same. It had never occurred to me that the rump of the turkey could become a highly charged emotional issue associated with mortality. But on this past Thanksgiving the rump and I connected in a poignant way.

This was the first Thanksgiving in thirty years that my

parents were not present in my home for dinner. Last year they joined us, but the steps leading into my house had proved challenging and painful, both psychologically and physically. And although I had taken pains to make the meal accessible for them, the crowd of twenty-five people limited the options.

Eating buffet style was difficult, and even with individual tables, my parents were sensitive to the frailties that age had imposed. Their shaking hands made eating somewhat embarrassing, and the location of the bathroom on the second floor caused an evening-long anxiety for all of us, since the climb was impossible. So this year, Mom and Dad discussed the situation and made the decision not to join us. I understood their concerns and agreed with their choice.

The anxieties I had become accustomed to when they visited were gone. No worry about the steps. No worry about the bathroom. No worry about transportation. Right choice. Realistic.

Then I began to carve the turkey. Mom and I have always shared the turkey rump, a high-cholesterol delicacy that we both relish. This time it was all mine. And as I loaded the table with traditional dishes, I thought back to the very first Thanksgiving I celebrated as a new wife. I remembered my mother's comment that she was excited to be eating her daughter's first turkey. This year for the thirtieth time, I put out the sweet potatoes with pineapple, brown sugar, and marshmallows . . . her recipe.

But it was the right decision, I reassured myself.

The guests came, each adding a special dish to the overloaded table. The food was steaming hot and the house smelled wonderfully of celebration. A toast to good health and good friends, and the buffet was served.

But when it came my turn to fill my plate, I couldn't take the rump. Somehow it didn't feel right. I missed sharing it. In a way that I had not expected at all, I suddenly missed my mother. I reminded myself that she was just down the road. But I also realized that in the mundane activities of my life, there are and will be a thousand things that evoke unexpected feelings, long forgotten memories, and unrecognized connections with my parents.

The turkey rump was a strange messenger of mortality and only the first of many that I am guessing I will meet. As our parents age, we may have to give up many traditions in preparation for the ultimate separation.

But somehow it is reassuring to know that the years of sharing inconsequential everyday experiences can lay a foundation that is nurturing and sustaining.

9

"Am I becoming my parents?"

TRADING PLACES

Telephones link all our lives in surprising ways. The phone I am holding rings monotonously as I wait for one of my parents to answer. Since they moved into the nursing home, I no longer panic when their phone rings for the tenth time and no one answers. When they were struggling to maintain themselves in their apartment, my heart rate would increase with each unanswered ring as I envisioned them in need of help and unable to call.

Finally I hear someone struggling to pick up the receiver and the script begins to play itself out. It is almost always the same script—comforting in its familiarity, sometimes humorous in its predictability, always reassuring because it lets me know that they are OK.

Since I usually call in the evening when I get home from work, the first thing I hear once the ringing stops is the sound of the news on television. My mother, despite being hard of hearing, is determined to keep up with the news, and so Dan Rather's voice is often more audible than my father's.

It is very difficult for either of my parents to walk now, and I find myself holding my breath as one of them struggles to the television set to lower the volume. Their set is a large old one and has no remote controls. Sometimes I think ridiculous thoughts as I wait until we can hear each other: "It'll be my fault if Dad falls because of this phone call." Sometimes I hear my mother yell a warning to my father, "Mick, use your walker! Be careful, please!" and my heart starts racing again. Sometimes, my father will answer and it will take my mother endless minutes and considerable pain before she can reach the phone to pick up.

Finally, everyone is seated and connected and we share each other's day. Ours is a venerable relationship, we've been talking with each other for more than fifty years. So the conversation feels very familiar. They ask me if I worked today. I ask them how their day went. They ask me how the kids are. I ask them if anything exciting happened. They ask me how my husband is. I ask them if they talked with any of their friends today. They ask me if we've eaten dinner yet. I ask them what they did today. They worry. I reassure. They share a new ache or pain. I worry. And so it goes.

Mundane, daily calls are interspersed with good news when there is some. Their granddaughter is getting ready for a college semester in Ireland. We talk about it. A grandson is nearing graduation from medical school. We anticipate it together. Another grandson is beginning an exciting research project in graduate school. We discuss his research. Always, the goal is to stay connected to one another and to fortify their connection to the rest of the world.

But lately a strange thing has begun to happen. The phone rings late at night. I answer. It's one of my children calling from college. I call to my husband who gets on the other line. Sometimes it takes him a minute or two to get to our second phone. And as our child and I wait, withholding conversation until we are all connected, I think to myself, "This feels familiar." And I wonder, listening to the sound of my son's breathing, what he is thinking. Am I becoming my parents?

10

"Anger is a healthy, normal, allowable feeling. . . .
I just don't know what to do with it."

FEELING MY FEELINGS

I don't like what I am beginning to feel. My mother reminded me for the fifth time to buy her a bottle of her favorite cologne and it made me angry. I'm over fifty, the mother of three adults, a professional, and I don't need my mother to tell me what I need to do. And yet I understood her focus and her concern. In the hectic run of my life, I can often forget what she and my father ask me to do. But resentment bubbled into my voice and I let it be heard.

I am their conduit to the outside world. I purchase the "quality of life" items that a nursing home cannot be expected to provide: photo albums, cologne, clothing, and so forth. As the circumference of my parents' world narrows and they become more self-focused, the circumference of mine is exploding outward in a middle-aged big bang that includes concern for them as well as for my husband, children, friends, and new job. Lately my time seems prioritized into two categories: critical and less critical. Cologne is not on my critical list. It is on my mother's. We get annoyed.

What do we do with these normal human feelings that we and our parents have about each other? How do you express anger to someone who is old and frail? I often feel, as designated caretaker, that I am walking on a razor's edge of guilt.

It's not hard to be angry with elderly parents who are making inconvenient demands upon you. The feelings come unbidden like spring water bubbling up from a natural source. I understand that these are healthy, normal, allowable feelings. I just don't know what to do with them. Each time a new situation arises I go through an emotional cost-benefit analysis. Do I get angry and yell? Do I try to sit down and explain? Do I stuff the feelings into a pathological pocket that will empty itself once they are gone? Do I vent to my husband or a friend? I've tried each with uneven success, and I've come to believe that the healthiest thing I can do for both my parents and myself is to acknowledge my right to feel these feelings and decide on an individual case basis what to do about them.

And each time I feel the resentment building, I try to remember a conversation I had with my mother several years ago. We were walking down the long hallway of her senior citizens' apartment building toward the elevator. Her pace had slowed considerably over the years, and now she was walking haltingly, using a cane and leaning periodically against the narrow hallway walls to catch her breath and rest. She was angry with herself and frustrated by her loss of vigor. "I remember," she began, "how it used to really annoy me when I walked with my mother and she walked so slowly and shuffled her feet. Now," she continued, "I can understand what she must have felt like."

Was she telling me that she understood what I was feeling as the daughter of an aging mother? Or was she saying that she now understood her mother better? Over the years since that walk, I have mentally played with this conversation. Slowing my pace to accompany my mother never bothered me. There are other different things that trigger my anger and resentment. And yet I felt a strange kinship with my mother once she confided that she felt guilty about how angry she had been with her mother. At some level, I think she was giving me permission to feel my feelings. I didn't need the permission, but I really appreciated that it was given.

11

"There is no blueprint to follow."

FAMILY COMMUNICATIONS

The work is piling up. My brother and I sat across from each other at my kitchen table, the two-inch-high stack of our parents' medical bills and statements between us. I apologized for the delay in collecting this information and getting it to him. He admitted to being intimidated at the size of the pile. We were both trying to be honest with each other and still not hurt or offend. We were traveling pathways of communication that had been laid down decades before when we were children in our parents' home. But we were following the road into new territory.

When adult children assume responsibility for the care of frail and aging parents, there is no blueprint to follow. The only constant is the parents' immediate and overwhelming need for oversight and help. Each family has to construct its own shelter out of the same bricks: the need for meals, help with personal hygiene, handling of finances, transportation, communication with doctors, and so on.

And like architects, each family must take certain stresses into account when designing its plan: the relationship parents have with each other and with their children, sibling relationships, who lives in town, who lives out of town, who can do what.

My brother and I have been at this for more than a year now. Until recently, he lived out of state and the bricks he could handle were limited. When he moved nearby we tried to assemble the pile of needs and place each brick in a way that would distribute them as evenly as possible. I'm doing financial and legal, he's doing medical and shopping. We both do transportation and doctors' visits when we can. My parents, who had until now depended on me for all of their needs, had to readjust their focus to include my brother as a resource.

Negotiations are delicate and even strong relationships can be challenged. Over time, there are hundreds of bricks that need to be placed. And the mortar that holds each brick in place and strengthens the shelter is a family's ability to share ideas and feelings, to listen to each other with respect and openness. Some families do it better than others.

My brother and I, our parents, and our families struggle with this daily. We have had successes. We have had failures. Our goal is to design a shelter in which we all feel comfortable, safe, and cared for. Like Californians, we are building along fault lines that are buried, that we cannot always see. We can only hope that we are placing each brick in a way that can withstand the shifting of the invisible plates on which we are living together.

12

"Things I didn't know . . ."

LEARNING THE DRILL

What I don't know—can hurt me. April 15 is a time of life review for most of us . . . an accounting of what we have done, where we have been, what we have earned, and how much a year of life has cost us. This year, when I was preparing my parents' income tax forms, reviewing their expenses and accounting for their finances, I stopped to think about all the new things I had to learn when they entered the nursing home and I began to take over the administration of their lives.

Armed with my power of attorney, I became their paper persona. I was their checkbook, I was their certificates of deposit, I was their social security checks, I was a letter to their lawyer and insurance companies, I was the administrator of their health care. And there was so much I needed to understand! I began a list of the things I didn't know. And even though some items on this list embarrass me because I should have known what to do and how to do it, I decided to share the list in the hope that my näiveté and/or ignorance might be of comfort to fellow travelers. I didn't know

- that all clothing in a nursing home must be labeled with the resident's name in waterproof ink
- what a power of attorney was
- what a durable power of attorney for health care was or how it is the same as or different from an advanced directive
- how to arrange an irrevocable trust for funeral expenses
- how to manage my parents' certificates of deposit
- how to balance their checkbook
- that patients in nursing homes must purchase and receive all their medications from the one pharmacy with which the home has an arrangement
- that medications may be prescribed for my parents and given to them without my being notified, so that when the bill for medicines comes, I have never heard of half of what is being administered
- the difference between Medicare and Medicaid
- how and when to apply for Medicaid
- that it would be crucial to have documentation of all my parents' expenses, assets, and liabilities for thirty-six months before they could be eligible to apply for Medicaid

- that there is a weekly large-print edition of the *New York Times* available for those who are visually impaired
- that if medication is prescribed for a nursing home resident and the resident refuses the medication, the resident is charged for each refused dosage until the doctor discontinues the medication, because once offered it cannot be returned to the pharmacy
- that reliable regular transportation for the frail elderly to doctors' appointments and hospital treatments is difficult to find and very expensive to keep
- that there are such people as elder law attorneys who specialize in issues involving senior citizens and help with such nightmares as preparing an application and documentation for Medicaid
- that in our county each nursing home has an ombudsman who represents the interests of the nursing home residents
- that checks received from insurance companies for medical coverage could be forwarded directly to doctors by writing "pay to the order of . . ." on the back of the check and signing my name followed by the words "power of attorney"
- that for a fee, nursing homes will send a staff member in a cab to accompany a resident to a doctor's appointment if family members cannot provide this help

- how to read and understand form messages from doctors, hospitals, and Medicare that begin with the statement "This Is Not a Bill"
- how to understand the actual bill
- the difference between face value and cash surrender value of life insurance policies
- what considerations need to be addressed when selecting a casket for someone else
- how it feels to do the above
- that nursing home residents can and do develop and nurture a sense of community among themselves

Far from being bliss, I have often found ignorance both uncomfortable and embarrassing. But I have also discovered that by not asking "stupid" questions I can invite even more painful consequences.

13

"These are not feelings I expected or wanted to have."

LEARNING THE HARD WAY

"When did you get home?" my mother asked. She was annoyed with me because I hadn't called her as soon as I got back into town. Since we've known each other for more than fifty years, I can translate her subliminal messages fairly well, and the message was clear, "You didn't do what you were supposed to, and you worried me."

Resentment rose as I explained that I had returned from West Virginia after she was asleep and had left for a meeting that next morning before she was awake. "Why am I explaining this?" I wondered. "I'm an adult and my mother doesn't need to know where I am every minute."

When we become the bottom line for our parents as they age into dependence, we often become the call button they push when they have physical and/or emotional needs. How to respond? I wrestle with that question many times in the course of each day, sorting through feelings and looking for an understanding that will help me cope better.

And I have had many unexpected emotions during my twelve-month journey.

I have been afraid

. . . when the phone rings and I recognize the voice of one of the nurses in the nursing home. My parents both have fallen many times. My father has gone into cardiac arrest and been revived. My mother has gone into diabetic shock.

. . . when I had to face the enormously complicated application process for Medicaid and the mounds of paperwork involved in managing two lives in addition to my responsibilities as wife and mother.

I have been happy

. . . when I have been able to help my parents improve

the quality of their lives in some way, like discovering a way to help stabilize books that they are too shaky to manage.

. . . when I see my father working with the two high school students who come weekly to help him lovingly create the scrapbooks and albums that are so vital to maintaining his intellect.

. . . when I see nursing home staff treat my parents with care and respect.

. . . when my family and I can celebrate milestones with my parents—birthdays, holidays, graduations.

I have been angry

. . . when I have had to deal with bureaucratic screwups involving my parents' finances, insurance, and bills as well as my own.

. . . when my parents have made what I consider unreasonable demands on me.

I have been frustrated

. . . when my responsibilities to my parents conflict with my obligations to my family.

. . . when I cannot convince my parents to try things I think might help them: like books on tape or taking regular physical therapy.

. . . when I cannot make things better for them, when I cannot fix what is wrong.

I have been sad

. . . when I see my parents deal with the challenges of

being basically confined to one room with one another day in and day out.

. . . when I see them losing ground physically as they struggle to maintain their vitality.

I have been lonely

. . . when I can no longer share my needs with my parents because they are too fragile emotionally to be helpful.

. . . when I struggle with feeling overwhelmed by their needs.

I have felt exhausted

. . . by the relentlessness of their needs. Just when I finish processing one pile of bills and records, another appears.

. . . by the unpredictability of their conditions: "Your father needs an MRI scan." "Your mother fell and was taken to the hospital with suspected broken ribs."

I have felt guilty

. . . sometimes when I am enjoying myself and doing things like eating whatever I want whenever I want. Institutional cooking has disappointed my parents even though the nursing home has made efforts to honor their requests for certain foods.

. . . when their paperwork piles up on my desk and I opt to go to a movie with my family on the weekend instead of getting current.

. . . when I put my needs before theirs.

But most of all, I have felt responsible.

. . .

And as I struggle with all of these conflicting feelings, I have turned to family and friends for advice, for a place to vent, for guidance, and for support. Like counterweights, they have helped balance the seesaw of feelings. When my husband validates my frustration or a friend talks about the difference between feeling guilty and feeling responsible, I recognize that I am learning and growing. These are not feelings I ever expected or wanted to have. These are not lessons for which I could have prepared. And yet these are lessons that most of us will face.

14

"There is no written law that says
family members will all love one another."

TRAVELING WITH FAMILY BAGGAGE

Loving each other can be hard sometimes. We often carry a great deal of baggage on the journey we take with our parents into their old age: suitcases full of old anger, childhood guilt, adult frustration, fractured relationships, less than perfect communications.

The luggage belongs to us, to our parents, to our siblings, to our spouses, to our children, all piled high on one vehicle heading into unknown territory. Some families travel lighter than others, but I know of no family that has not packed for the trip.

For me, the goal was to slowly get rid of as much extra weight as I could when I first saw my parents growing older, more frail, and more dependent. As a very late-blooming adolescent, I carried much of the normal rebellion and anger of my youth well into middle age. But at some point, my parents' growing dependence bumped up against my ability to finally reach a healthy separation from them. It was a moment of truth.

Recognizing the feelings of resentment that often came along with their increased need of me, I found several wise and wonderful friends with whom to process these emotions. But as my parents' needs grew, there were other feelings to be dealt with . . . and they were not mine.

Till recently, my brother lived out of state and this limited our ability to share the load of increasing parent care. When he moved to this area, we divided responsibilities and talked about the strain these growing needs were having on us individually, as brother and sister, and in our separate families. There is an entire set of feelings, unfamiliar to me, that an out-of-state sibling has to process when parents need care. Through my brother, I came to understand this.

When mothers and fathers have to care for *their* mothers and fathers, the time and energy must be drawn from somewhere. Often it is at the expense of time spent with spouse and children. And it is at this very point in our own middle-aged lives that most of us clearly begin to hear the clock ticking down the time *we* have remaining. The pressure to hoard this precious resource begins to creep into our thinking and feelings. For each of us caring for a frail elder parent, there is that constant search for the point of balance that will allow us to best meet everyone's needs, including our own.

Our children and spouse may be supportive, helpful, and caring, but I think they often miss us when we are unavailable to them and focused on our parents. And they may be reluctant to tell us for fear of making our job more difficult. For those married couples with more confrontational relationships, their spouses and children may be very clear about resenting the imposition on family life.

There is no written law that says family members will all love one another. There is no mandate forcing them to understand, to share, or even to care. There is no guarantee of help. Each family responds according to its history. These are the suitcases that are strapped to the roof of the car we are in.

Yet in the absence of laws, mandates, or guarantees, families have to negotiate this journey. And as we often fumble to communicate painful feelings with each other, we hope we can complete the trip strengthened rather than weakened.

For this kind of traveling, there is no scale with which to weigh our baggage before we embark. And I think perhaps this is a good thing. We have to go regardless of what we are carrying. But as with any kind of travel, it costs us more to carry extra weight. I guess the secret of a satisfying trip is to arrive at the departure station packed light.

PART II

Evening

Losses

Evening for my parents is filled with losses. Darkness comes slowly over a long period of time. Their ability to care for themselves increasingly fades as illness robs them of control over their bodies. Walking, writing, hearing, seeing, tasting, and reading become things of the past. As their failing senses cut them off from the rest of the world, isolation and loneliness set in.

I find that I cannot fill the gaping holes in their lives, but I am driven to try. Their physical pain becomes my mental agony. How can I make their days better? What have I not thought of? What more can I do? Their grief and depression become mine as we mourn together. Along with their losses come my own: loss of time, loss of focus on family and work, loss of balance in life. Moments of pleasure and solitude are tinged with feelings of guilt. It is difficult to live joyfully.

My parents get angry at the world, at themselves, at each other, at their caretakers, at me. I resent their feelings at the same time as I struggle to meet their needs. We often race in endless circles, chasing problems that have no solutions, seeking answers where often there are none. Powerful feelings of fear, anger, love, and hate wage war as we struggle together and with each other.

And in the midst of this maelstrom, I am looking for closure with my parents before it is too late. There are good things I need to tell them. There are important things I want to hear. The time for blame is past. Love becomes painful to express because it feels like good-bye. We do it anyway.

15

"We do the elderly a terrible disservice
when we forget who they were when they were strong."

LOOKING BACKWARD AND FORWARD

It was 1:30 A.M. on a Sunday morning when the dusty old shoe box caught my eye. It had been on an upper bookcase shelf since my parents moved some eighteen months ago. Now it was mine. In my father's distinctive handwriting it said "spare pictures."

I opened it gingerly. Inside were photographs I had never seen before: of my parents when they were young, of now elderly cousins in their infancy, of aunts and uncles now gone. Always the album keeper, my father had stowed these away for one reason or another in a nondescript box. Perhaps they didn't meet his standards for a photograph well taken. Or maybe he felt he already had enough photos of this or that person.

I fingered through them carefully so as not to flake away the yellowed brittle edges of the oldest ones. They must have dated back to the 1930s—my father as an adolescent Boy Scout, shirtless, his rippled muscles reflecting summer sunlight. My mother, dark haired, slender, laughingly hiding in the arms of a tall man I had never seen before. My mother and father together, arms around each other, in their twenties . . . handsome . . . pretty . . . happy.

I must have spent more than an hour slowly exploring the contents of that box, thinking, "That was then . . . this is now." It wasn't sadness that came, but a clearer understanding of how quickly time passes and at what cost.

I'm not sure, but I'm willing to guess that each of us has imprinted in our minds a picture of how our parents looked physically as we grew up and then grew older alongside them. Their hands, their arms, their hair. At forty, at fifty, at seventy. My mother is old and her hands are thin and gnarled. The veins stand out in a kind of lavender bas-relief. But I remember how they looked when I was twenty-two and getting married. I remember when her wedding ring wasn't loose and didn't slip up and down her finger. Was she ever really the coquettish dark-haired beauty in another man's arms, the image of whom is now tinged sepia with the passage of time?

My father's fingers have always been long and slender, capped by rock-hard nails. I looked at his arms in the photographs. They looked young and supple and strong. Today he is fragile and his hands are mottled with the entropy of age. But here, in black and white, he is young, taut bellied, and mustached.

I found myself wondering what they had been like before I was born. Obviously they were both handsome people. Their faces looked expectant, excited, hopeful. What had been their dreams? I felt strange trying to relate those faces, those bodies, those expressions to the elderly parents I now knew. And I felt compelled to remember that today they still have within them the memories and experiences of their youth. In the time before me, who were they?

We do the elderly a terrible disservice when we forget who they were when they were strong. Despite all her frailties, my mother's eyes can still snap with the sharpness of a keen mind. And in my father I see glimmers of the young man who was fascinated by airplanes and science and flight. I tell myself I must not only try to know who they are, but also remember who they were. My father's photographs have given me a better frame of reference.

And of course, I look at my hands, and my hair, and I see changes that frighten me. Not because I'm afraid of growing older, but because I'm afraid of growing irrelevant.

16

"I had become temporarily old."

LOSING INDEPENDENCE

Illness links my parents and me. Returning home from the hospital after recent surgery, I looked at the plastic identification bracelet around my wrist and thought of my parents. As residents of a nursing home, my mother and father wear similar bracelets. For the past five days we had shared more than the bracelet. I felt as if I had stepped into their skins, and the experience was very unsettling.

Awakening in the recovery room following abdominal

surgery, I was struck by the irony of my situation. I had become temporarily old. Moving was painful and slow. I needed help with almost everything. I could not walk unassisted. Someone had to bring me food, and dietary decisions had been made without my input.

I evaluated all efforts in terms of physical cost. How badly did I really want the tissues that were just out of my reach? My independence had diminished and my world had narrowed to the hospital room and hallway. Television was more than just entertainment, the telephone more than just a convenience. They were connections to the rest of the world. I had become my parents.

The more I lay in bed and thought about it, the stronger the parallels became. Washing was exhausting. Intercom announcements interrupted concentration and sleep. Dressing and undressing became a marathon of frustration and endurance. "How do they manage?" I wondered. And human contact meant so much! Company and phone calls made me feel valued and nurtured. Flowers, cards, and balloons were constant reminders that I mattered to someone.

I kept asking myself, "Is this what it's like for them? What can I do to make it easier?" The answer left me feeling empty. "Not much," I thought. I can visit, phone, send cards, and bring gifts. But I can do little to help them combat their growing dependency on others.

And a part of me felt guilty. I was getting better. I was going to heal. I would be stronger following surgery. They are not going to improve. They are fighting merely to maintain.

I cut the identity bracelet from my wrist and dropped it in the trash can, feeling that I was shedding both age and illness. I thought about the saying, "Don't talk the talk till you walk the walk," and now I knew what it meant. I had walked the walk and it frightened me. I had become temporarily old. My parents are permanently old. And I am moving in their direction.

17

"I walk like Frankenstein."

INVISIBLE INDIGNITIES

Mom and Dad are losing ground. Recently I came face-to-face with two of the invisible indignities of old age, and the lesson was painful. We are all probably familiar with the losses we can see in our parents: the loss of muscle tone, the loss of some bodily functions, the loss of alertness. But often the elderly experience a loss only they are aware of: the loss of dignity.

On a Sunday afternoon I visited my parents. My father's youngest sister, who is seventy, was also visiting. We reminisced about collective family memories, and my aunt shared some of her feelings about approaching old age. "I hate to look in the mirror," she confided, and my parents nodded in silent agreement.

When it was time to go to the dining room for dinner, my father rose to prepare himself: tuck in his shirt, comb his hair. I watched as he struggled out of the chair and began to cross the room without his walker. He walked slowly, stiffly, and very unsteadily toward my mother's wheelchair. "I walk like Frankenstein," he said with a self-deprecating laugh and an apologetic look toward his sister.

It pained me to see how much his awkward walking embarrassed him. I thought about this assault on his sense of dignity and flinched inwardly. When we are young, the way we walk says a great deal about us as individuals. Some of us have a vigorous purposeful walk, others may lope along, bounce, or glide fluidly. Our walk can change as often as our need to move, but each of us has a signature stance and gait. Many elderly people, though, seem to lose that lifelong individualizing characteristic as their bodies age. As illness and atrophy blend, walking becomes a kind of communal shuffling. I hadn't realized before how my father felt about the way he walks now.

With my mother, the indignity was even more obscure. My son recently graduated from medical school, and with the help of family and friends, my parents were able to attend the graduation party held at my home.

My mother had planned far in advance what she would wear, so I knew it was an important event for her. She was very nicely dressed when she arrived. But she wore no lipstick and so looked very pale and drawn. I remember thinking that lipstick would have made such a big difference. Maybe she was depressed, I thought, and just didn't want to bother.

It was only a week later that she mentioned in casual conversation that she was no longer able to apply lipstick because her hands shake too much. Once again, I flinched.

Had I known, I would have offered to put it on for her when she came to the party.

There are, of course, more visible indignities that the elderly experience involving personal care and the need for help. But I think that many endure losses that we never recognize. I thought my mother didn't care that she looked so pale. I was wrong.

18

"I just told my father why he couldn't walk."

MAKING CHOICES

Bad news is hard to share. I envy my computer. Somewhere in its electrical complexity is something called a "chooser," and I wish I had one. I'd push a button and all the pros and cons would be weighed. All the negatives and positives would be evaluated, all the fors and againsts would be calculated. And then the decision would be made for me.

I just spent two hours telling my father what his doctor said about why he was losing his ability to walk. My father has some heavy choosing to do, and I wish there were a button I could push to make it easier for him. How do you help elderly parents make difficult decisions?

I don't think there is a clearly right or wrong way. I search for a way that is comfortable, a way that feels OK to me—a process to help them decide that is congruent with my values and philosophy and also recognizes theirs. For me this means that when my parents are faced with difficult decisions, I feel responsible for helping them see and understand all of the options. The decision, however, is theirs to make. If asked, I will volunteer my opinion. Otherwise I try hard to remove myself. In this case, it is important that my dad own both the decision and its consequences. The quality of his life, even his life itself, hangs in the balance.

Although at eighty-one my father is very frail, his intellect is intact and he still does many of the things that he loves: reading, making scrapbooks to document historic events, listening to music, writing.

His doctor called me to explain that the difficulty Dad has experienced lately in walking is due to a narrowing in the opening in his spinal column. The condition may be correctable by surgery that involves the removal of bone. My father is a terrible surgical risk, and the doctor was very careful to explain to me all the various options he saw, trying to eliminate his own personal bias. I repeated the process with my father.

For two hours we talked about his continued attempts to walk and his continued experiences falling. We talked about the prognosis—paraplegia and incontinence. We talked about quality of life with or without the surgery. With all of his medical complications, surgery poses a real threat to my father's intellect. His circulatory system, heart, and remaining kidney are very fragile, and even the slightest dip in blood pressure, common during a surgical procedure, could result in a loss of mental ability. We talked about pain. Without the surgery, although limited to a wheelchair, the doctor believes that my father will be relatively pain free. We talked on and on. The process drained us.

In the end, my father decided to seek input from a specialist, an orthopedist or neurosurgeon, before making a final decision. This made sense to me and I said I would arrange it. My father didn't ask me what he should do, he asked me what I thought. I thought gathering more information was reasonable. If and when he asks me what I think he should do, I will have a hard time answering. I can only answer for myself. I can only answer based on what is important to me in my own life. As my father weighs life in a wheelchair and incontinence against the risks of surgery, only he can decide what is important to him.

I am blessed by the fact that both of my parents are alert and able to make these decisions. If and when these decisions become mine to make on their behalf, the responsibility will become heavier. I think again about the chooser in my computer and realize that choosing quality of life is a very intimate and human experience. It is not black and white. It is not right or wrong. It is not off or on. It cannot be counted or quantified. It is personal, private, and protected from techniques and technology. My father's decision is not mechanical, it is spiritual. It is what makes us human. And sometimes it is hard and very painful.

19

"I can't see their faces. . . . I can't hear. I can't taste."

LOSSES

Mom is losing it. She leaned toward me with an unusual expression on her face. "You know," she confided, "I am so embarrassed. When the nurses come into my room, I don't recognize them. I know they must think I'm crazy."

It took me a moment to realize that what I was reading on my mother's face was humiliation and frustration. "Why don't you recognize them?" I asked, and opened a door that has taken me on another unexpected journey.

"I can't see their faces," Mom responded. "All I can see is a blur. The only way I can tell who they are is if I recognize the shape of their hairstyle. Some of them recently got haircuts and now I never know who it is, except for one nurse. I recognize a necklace she always wears."

I knew Mom had been having trouble with her eyes. A cataract operation had not helped and she still had trouble reading and watching television. But I did not know about the social problems she was having. Trips to a local ophthalmologist had left us without any clear answers. So I made an appointment with a specialist at the Johns Hopkins Wilmer Eye Institute.

It was a long drive over and we munched on McDonald's and reminisced about my childhood on the way. Once there,

Mom had her eyes dilated. And as we sat for a long time waiting for the drops to take effect, she began a painful inventory of the failings of her body. "I can't hear well at all. I can't taste anything. I have no feeling in my hands and feet because of neuropathy, so I can't walk. I have constant back pain. And I can't see. I think it might be better just to let me go," she said.

I looked at her sitting in the long corridor in her wheelchair—a frail, thin, white-haired woman with snapping brown eyes. It was the snapping eyes that held me.

"Mom," I countered, "would it make a difference if you could read again?" I could see the feistiness and spirit rekindle. It was like blowing on a fading ember. She thought before she responded. "Yes, of course it would make a difference," she answered with an anger not directed at me.

I suddenly realized that being unable to read the newspaper or a favorite novel, and being unable to watch the news on television had disconnected my mother from the world. A lifelong reader, she was used to whizzing through novels and poring over the paper each day. And loss of hearing was further isolating her. One thing at a time, I warned myself, and I made a commitment to follow her vision problems to an answer.

The specialist at Johns Hopkins advised against immediate laser surgery and referred us to an optometrist—a low vision specialist—who was especially good with elderly patients. We went and he was. This wonderfully patient man listened to my mother describe her problems. He spoke loudly when she explained that she was hard of hearing. He spoke directly to her and put her in charge of her medical decisions. His language was clear and jargon free. And he responded to her priority.

"I want to get you reading," he explained, "and we'll work with one eye at a time." He introduced my mother to lighted magnifiers, lap desks, and other equipment designed to optimize reading ability. He spent two hours juggling lenses and responding to my mother's physical condition. "You can't hold a magnifier because your hand shakes? Okay, you can hang one around your neck."

When my mother became tired or despondent, he reminded her that the glass was half full, not half empty. He assured her that she had enough vision left to be able to read. And like an alchemist mixing and matching, he arrived at a pair of glasses, with one lens frosted, that would allow her to read using only her right eye. "We'll work on the left eye also, but you need to see a retina specialist, so we'll do this one step at a time," the doctor told my mother.

We have seen the retina specialist and been advised of different laser procedures that might be helpful. But all of the doctors must confer with each other now, and so we are left with no alternative but to be patient and persistent.

Reading is still difficult for my mother. New things are hard for her. She is reading a weekly large-print edition of the *New York Times* and she just finished an exciting mystery novel. She is back in the world. And I explained her vision problem to the staff at the nursing home, suggesting that perhaps they could announce themselves by name when they visit her room.

The medical appointments are hard to fit into my work

life, the wheelchair is difficult to get in and out of the car, and Mom and I are both exhausted by these journeys. But instead of banking the fire and allowing it to fade, I feel as if together we have thrown another log into the fireplace and rekindled the flame.

20

"Isn't holding a book hard for you?"

INNOVATING AROUND LOSSES

Sometimes I surprise myself. Who would have believed that the flute lessons my daughter took twelve years ago would have an impact today upon my mother's ability to read? It's a long and winding road from one to the other, but the ending is a happy one.

This week, we went back to the ophthalmologist for a regular checkup and he confirmed that Mom's vision had improved considerably under the care of several specialists. She should be able to read with more ease. However, it was puzzling to all three of us that reading was still so difficult for her.

In a quiet aside to me, the doctor suggested that perhaps my mother didn't like to wear her thick, heavy reading glasses. Knowing Mom to be very pragmatic, I ruled this out. Consideration of beauty would never replace the intellectual stimulation she enjoyed when reading a good book.

I asked her immediately if wearing her glasses bothered her, and she snapped back, "Of course not!"

The doctor, Mom, and I began to brainstorm, trying to think of what was keeping her from reading. Suddenly I had one of those moments of clarity. "Mom," I suggested, "isn't holding a book hard for you? Your hands shake so much and your arms get tired."

"Yes . . . ," she responded almost with a question mark at the end. "Even leaning over a book placed on your bed tray is hard for you, isn't it?" I pursued. "Yes," she agreed once again.

And then the doctor joined in the sleuthing. "You know," he said, "earlier today I had an eighty-six-year-old patient who was using a music stand to help hold books and newspapers so that he could read."

Bingo! "Mom," I almost shouted. "I have one at home! I have a music stand that Amy used when she took flute lessons!"

Needless to say, when I got home, I tore my basement apart until I found the stand buried in a pile of debris that had been undisturbed for more than a decade. I took it to Mom the next day.

Carefully erecting it (I am challenged by any machinery more complicated than a pencil) I pulled the stand over to Mom's chair and placed a large-print *Reader's Digest* on it. By positioning the stand between her knees, she could pull the book up close to her and adjust the height. It worked! She was able to read—even without her glasses!

It had never occurred to me that for an elderly person, the ability to read can depend upon more than just vision. It can depend on physical comfort: reading while leaning over a table hurts Mom's back. It can depend on a stationary text: books and papers held in hands that shake are hard to read. It can depend on keeping the pages open: the music stand has two flexible holders to keep pages in place. So, I guess reading is like a recipe . . . you need to have all the necessary ingredients to make it work.

I even had a second line of attack, if the music stand didn't work: a wooden stand for needlework that has a magnifying glass attached. "Very creative," the ophthalmologist enthused. "I think we're on the right track!"

When my dad saw how the music stand worked, he immediately realized it could help him as well. Since his stroke, his left hand has been numb and curled into a fist. Holding a large book has been awkward and difficult. Forestalling any competition for the stand, I offered to get another one for him. "No," he responded, "we'll share this one for now and see how it works out." I left the nursing home feeling triumphant.

Necessity truly is the mother of invention. And I am left wondering what other innovative, creative, hidden ingredients I can uncover to make the journey into old age more comfortable and more meaningful for my parents.

21

"I absolutely and totally love what this wild act represented."

A GOOD LOSS

I can't imagine what made him do it. Was it reckless abandon at eighty-one? Was it accidental? Was it symbolic of rebellion, a kind of Johnny-come-very-lately adolescence? My father shaved off his mustache!

Now, you need to understand that I have only seen my father's upper lip once in the fifty-three years I have known him, and that happened when I was four and lasted for only a day. I remember it because we have a photograph.

Let me back up a moment and relive my first impression of this recent shock. Last week I visited my parents. Knocking lightly, I was unprepared for what happened as I swung the door open and entered.

Dad had been napping and as he rose slowly to greet me, I looked at him and the words tumbled from my lips spontaneously. "Oh, my God," I found myself whispering. "Dad, what happened?!" With a sheepish grin (so uncharacteristic because without a mustache his whole face looked different), he said, "I just decided to do it."

As I sat down in astonishment, trying to adjust to this new old face, my mother entered the room and with her characteristic bluntness said, "Well, what do you think of your father's bald face?" The three of us dissolved into laughter.

Then I sat back and watched my father talk. It was fascinating to me. He looked totally different. All at once, I could see my brother's face mirrored in his. I never realized how much alike they look when they smile. There was just the hint of a dimple that had hidden behind that bushy handlebar for the past sixty-three years.

Sixty-three years. "Dad, what possessed you? How did you come to do this?" I asked in wonderment. "It just got too hard to keep it neat," he replied, still smiling in amusement at my reaction. "I grew a mustache when I was eighteen and now I'm eighty-one and it was time. Besides," he added, "all my uncles had mustaches for most of their lives, and they shaved them off when they got old."

"It makes you look so much younger," I said, and my mother piped up again. "Yes, someone said that now the nurses will be chasing him down the hallways." The uncharacteristic joshing among the three of us was so much fun.

I spent almost two hours visiting with my parents that afternoon, and for most of that time, my eyes were glued to my father's newly emerged upper lip. All of his expressions looked new to me. It was the same balding head, the same gray hair, the same brown eyes, the same family nose. But from the nose down, he was a stranger. The most extraordinary thing was his smile. It was almost as if he had been hiding it behind his mustache for all those years.

I thought of my two grown sons, who between adolescence and adulthood had rearranged their facial hair so often they were semi-strangers every week. They had gone from beards and mustaches, to beards alone, to mustaches alone, to clean-shaven without rhyme or reason, leaving sinks full of clippings behind. In their cases, I told myself that they were seeking comfortable adult identities. Eventually they each settled on an arrangement that met their needs and everyone's face became familiar again.

I wondered what my father had thought about as he removed this symbol of his entire adult life. Was this rebellion, frustration, experimentation, or an act of youthful longing? I'll never know because I'm not sure he'll ever know. But I absolutely and totally love what this wild act represented. Despite his many infirmities, with each swipe of the razor, he was choosing to live.

22

"My mother's wrists are getting thinner."

LIVING WITH HER CHOICES

Some things about Mom and Dad are beginning to frighten me. My mother's wrists are getting thinner and it worries me. Every time I visit my parents I do an eyeball evaluation of their well-being, and lately I have become very concerned about my mother's weight.

Never hefty to begin with, as a diabetic for the past forty years she has exercised a rigid and healthy control over her diet. But each time I look at her lately, she appears thinner and more frail. And she is not eating much at all. The situation needs attention, and I begin the journey down another new road.

I ease into the investigation. "Mom, you look like you may have lost weight." She tells me she has. "Are you eating OK?" She tells me she isn't. "Why? What's wrong?" She tells me the food tastes terrible. "Have you discussed this with the kitchen staff?" I ask. "Oh," she responds, "it's not the food. It's me," and goes on to explain a situation that is already familiar to me. As a longtime diabetic, my mother has lost the ability to taste most foods, and often what she eats tastes like ashes in her mouth, with the exception of something like a good strong pickle. "I'm eating, but only a little, only what I need to survive," she explains.

My mind flips into my mothering mode and I try to "fix it" for my mom. "Can I bring you some fruit to keep in your room?" No, she doesn't want any. "How about some really good crackers or maybe even those little cheese packages that don't need refrigeration." No again. A last try, "Can I bring you in a deli sandwich or maybe even some carryout you would enjoy." Nope. Nothing needed. And then I begin to understand.

Living in a body that is slowly losing its function, her will is the last remaining thing that my mother can truly control. She is losing her hearing. She is losing her vision. She is losing her ability to walk. She can no longer read or crochet. She is refusing to take physical therapy classes offered in the nursing home. She is choosing to sleep most of the day because her body now has such a hard time interacting with the rest of the world. And hard as it is, I need to respect both her right to choose and the choices she makes.

The same is true for my father. He is also making choices with which I do not agree. He has elected not to take physical therapy classes either. In the stubbornness so typical of his stoic ability to deal with adversity, he is often refusing to use his walker as he moves about his room. Unsteady as the result of his stroke, he continues to risk falling. I think it's because using the walker is inconvenient in their small room and because it makes him feel old. But I keep telling myself that these are his choices. He has the right to make them and the responsibility then to live with the consequences.

The hard part for me is that I also have to live with the consequences of their choices. Whatever happens to my parents becomes my responsibility to address. If my father falls, I have to deal with difficult logistics, with resultant medical bills, with supporting and nurturing him through another physical insult to an already battle-scarred body. And yet, I must do this. Not because I am a good daughter or an attentive nurturer. But because this control, this ability to decide what they will and will not do, is their life's blood. It is what primes the pump and keeps them both alive. For more than eighty years they have both made decisions about their bodies and their lives. Without my help. Without my input. I need to respect that. And I do.

23

"It never occurred to me that my mother would miss her handwriting."

LOSING CONTROL

It never occurred to me that my mother would miss her handwriting. Today she signed a graduation card for my son and it was painful for both of us: painful for her to try to control the shaking of her hand and painful for me to watch her struggle.

"Damn." She muttered under her breath as she formed each letter. "I miss being able to write." I was struck by the passion in her voice and her sense of loss.

We take our handwriting so much for granted, forgetting how very individualized it is. Handwriting is our paper persona. It is a unique, special, and personal presentation of ourselves. How often can we recognize the handwriting on a piece of mail before we read the return address? Recently I was rummaging through a pile of old papers and I came across a note that my father-in-law had written before he died. I think it was a shopping list. I could not throw it away because it was so tangibly a part of him.

Now I sat beside my mother and willed each letter to take form. And I had a sense of déjà vu. For years and years, my grandmother in New York wrote faithfully to her daughter in Washington. When I was a child her cards were impossible for me to read. The letters were jerky and jagged, written in lines that slanted unevenly. But my mother could translate them, and they always began with the same line, "Dear Evie, glad to hear that all is well . . ." This was my immigrant grandmother, who had learned to write in English specifically to write to my mother. She learned as an elderly woman, so her handwriting hadn't changed much over the years. It began squiggly and it stayed that way.

But my mother's writing is a different story. Until the past few years it was full and flowing, graceful and precise. As she aged and it began to change, I felt the loss. I never thought about how it affected her. So it surprised me to hear the anger in her voice. Whom does one rail against? She was angry at the body that was failing her. For a woman whose entire life was built around an appreciation for order and precision, this represented a loss of control that enraged her. Her muscles would no longer obey her will.

She looked critically at what she had written, "Love, Grandma and Grandpa." It had taken her several painful minutes to complete the line. Despite her persistence and full concentration, it was difficult to read. And yet I felt that it was important for my son to see her message, to know that she acknowledged his accomplishment. I only hoped, in reading the card, that he would recognize hers.

24

"Mmmmm, it even smells like Grandma."

THE MEANING OF THINGS

It was a serendipitous moment, a time when the puzzle pieces fit together with a satisfying "ker-chunk." My son had come home from graduate school for the weekend and was talking about the converted army barracks that would be his dormitory this fall. The only thing he knew about them, he volunteered, was that they would be very cold during the winter.

With the thrill of a veteran mother, I hurried to our storage closet and took down a warm, heavy, colorful afghan my mother had made and used as a bedspread. "Here," I held it out to him. "Grandma made this. It should help."

"Great! Thanks, Mom," my son said with enthusiasm, as he raised the soft blanket to his face. "Mmmmm, it even smells like Grandma," he murmured, inhaling deeply.

I smiled as I remembered my mother making this one. She had made two the same, in green and blue, one for her bed and one for my dad's. I can't remember back to when they didn't lie neatly folded at the foot of their beds. Moving into a nursing home requires parting with many cherished possessions. Mom had decided that the afghans were too heavy and too warm to take with her and gave them to me. So they joined the fifteen or so blankets she had crocheted for me over the years. But these were different; they weren't mine. They were Mom's and Dad's. They carried with them a different feeling. It was a feeling my son appreciated, and it made me glad to see them cherished and useful.

Pleased with myself for making this son-to-blanket match, I began to think about how some things take on a special meaning in our lives without our even realizing it. My mother can no longer crochet. Arthritis, poor vision, and diminishing strength in her hands (to tie all those knots) have put an end to the activity she enjoyed most in life. Everyone in the family has at least one of the blankets and baby buntings she has made to warm several generations. And she grieves this loss as if the skill had been a close friend, which it really was. It was her company on cold, snowy evenings. It was her consolation when worries beset her and she needed respite. It was her relaxation, her tranquilizer, her passion. Each blanket was her way of telling the recipients that they mattered. Speaking about love has never been easy for my mother. She let her fingers do the talking.

Some time ago, when she retired from working, Mom and I decided it would be really special for her to crochet three sets of baby buntings, afghans, carriage covers, and hats for each of my children to put away for their children. That way, Grandma Evelyn would be assured of being present at the birth and remembered. But, as it turns out, she doesn't have to wait that long for her work to be appreciated. Each of my children has her blankets on their beds in my home, in their dorm rooms, in their homes.

I think of all the years I watched her work, each square neatly pressed and laid in a box beside her chair with almost obsessive precision. Her fingers are idle now and her knitting bag stands unused beside her bed. I mourn the loss with her. And this week I had a particularly poignant moment with my daughter. She had taken photographs of the family and caught one of me at my recreation, my tranquilizer, my passion: needlework. And I looked around at the thirty-plus samplers I have fashioned and hoped that they would be as meaningful to my children as my mother's handiwork is to me. We have a joke in our family each time I make my kids pose for a photograph. "It'll be a memory," I cajole as they frown at being made to stop and be frozen in time. You never know what will become special.

25

"I'm bringing my mom her teeth."

A FULL PLATE

Laughter can definitely heal. So please travel with me through the misery of this story to the happy ending. Old age often is not funny, so I have savored this over the past week and called it up every once in a while to realign my perspective and make me chuckle.

The call came late at night after a particularly intense day at the office. I knew when my mother said, "Judy?" instead of hello that something was wrong. I braced myself for what was coming. "I broke my plate," she said in a voice that dripped with anger, frustration, and demand. "You'll have to get the dentist to fix it," she told me.

I didn't need to be told. The heaviness of how-am-I-going-to-fit-this-into-my-life descended upon me. I had an impending editing deadline, a staff meeting, and an hour-long conference call already on my plate for the following day. Getting Mom and her wheelchair to the dentist felt insurmountable on such short notice. I called my brother. He had meetings scheduled for several days that could not be changed.

It was 11 P.M. I called our dentist's office and left a message on his recorder. As a young dental student, Allan had arranged a blind date for me. It was with my husband. I owe Allan. "Allan, Mom broke her plate and is having difficulty eating. Because she's diabetic, this could be serious. Could you give me a call?" Having done all I could at that late hour, I went to bed and had a hard time sleeping.

Allan's office called early the next morning. He was out of town until the evening but would call as soon as he got in. I called Mom and she assured me she could eat well enough for a day. I went to work and plowed through my schedule.

Allan called that night. "Listen," he said comfortingly. "Don't bring your mom in, just bring the plate and let me see if I can repair it." Grateful, I agreed to get the plate to his office very early the next morning. That meant I needed to get to the nursing home to pick it up. It was already 9 P.M. I drove over. Both of my parents were asleep when I tiptoed into the room and began searching. I found it, listened to sleepy instructions from my mother about its care, and left with the broken treasure on the front seat of my car.

Early the next morning I dropped it off at Allan's. He promised to get on it quickly. We were fast approaching the weekend and I was leaving town to attend my daughter's college graduation. I had yet to buy a Mother's Day gift for Mom and so I set aside that final evening after work to shop. Allan called me Thursday at work. The plate was ready. My shopping time evaporated. Leaving work late, I raced to Allan's home. He had agreed to leave the plate on the front seat of his car because he was going to bed. It was dark as I approached his car, feeling like a thief, and opened the front door to retrieve the plate.

Driving to the nursing home I realized that I had to get home, wash clothes, pack, and load the car so that I could leave for graduation after work the next day. The nursing home had already locked its doors for the night, so I had to use a special entrance and explain to the nurses why I was there at that hour. "I'm bringing my mom her teeth," I said with a smile I hoped would convince them to let me in. They did and I raced up the steps to my parents' room carrying Mom's teeth in a plastic sandwich bag. She was up and expectant. With a sigh of relief, I handed her the bag. Once the plate was in and she had tested its comfort, we talked.

"Gee, Mom," I explained as I caught my breath. "I've been running around with your teeth for two days and now I don't have time to shop for Mother's Day before I leave for Amy's graduation tomorrow."

"Don't worry about it," she admonished me. I still felt terrible. I would be out of town on Mother's Day and now I didn't even have a gift! Then with a broad grin, I thought of the perfect solution. Holding up the empty plastic bag and pointing to her teeth, I leaned over, kissed Mom on the top of her head, and wished her a Happy Mother's Day. "At least this year you won't tell me I have to exchange the gift," I teased, recalling her penchant for being unhappy with the clothing I select for her. And for the first time in a long, long time, my mother laughed out loud.

26

"Setting those boundaries allows me to visit without resentment."

THE LIMITS OF CARE

I have a confession to make, and my guess is that it is no secret to my parents. At times, visiting them is not much fun. When they are feeling ill, when they are in pain, when they are frustrated and angry, my visits, I believe, distract them and disturb me.

I think that every child who has a parent in a nursing home has to negotiate with him or herself just what level of attention to a parent's needs is comfortable. Parents and adult children can differ on what makes each comfortable, how much is enough. I have known people who visit a parent in a nursing home every day. I know of others who visit much less often. And I have come to understand that it is unfair to measure love by how often one visits or calls.

I have come to a negotiated peace with myself. I speak

with my parents every day on the phone, a habit we established long before they entered a nursing home. I am very grateful that they are alert and able to do this. It gives me great comfort to be able to speak with them and know that they are OK. I try to visit them once a week. And in between the phone calls and the visit, I take care of their financial lives. This works for me. Setting these boundaries allows me to visit without resentment . . . most of the time.

But there are those moments when I would rather not, those times when I am struggling with a problem I choose not to share with them, those times when I know they are angry about something, those times when I am just exhausted and cannot muster the energy to meet their needs or reassure them. And then the visit is very hard.

Many people have shared with me their own difficulties dealing with a similar situation. Their sharing has helped me feel less guilty about some of my own feelings. And I want to return their generosity. We are human and these are human emotions. We have the right to feel them and then the responsibility to deal with them. And there is no right or wrong answer. The answer is, the answer changes with every individual.

27

"The telephone is both a blessing and a curse."

TRADING VOICE MAIL

Reading between the lines is not hard on the phone. When you know someone really well, your ear becomes a kind of auditory camera. I can usually tell by the way my mother answers the phone and says hello how she is feeling. I can tell when my father has had dialysis because the pitch of his voice becomes significantly higher. It has always amazed me how sensitive the auditory antennae are between parents and children. Especially over the telephone, when there are no visual cues.

I know when my parents are angry with each other and when they are angry with me. It's not the words that convey the message. It's the tone, the harshness and softness, the space between words. And I know they listen to every nuance of my voice when I call them, and they extract a picture of my day from what they hear.

When my parents entered the nursing home, the phone became a kind of lifeline. It took about a week to have it installed, and I was amazed to find out how much I missed talking with them while we waited. Once it was in place, my parents and I kind of took each other's temperatures daily through that instrument.

"You sound tired," my dad would say when I called after a hard day at work. "You sound down; is everything OK?"

they'd ask as they fine-tuned their thermometer. There are times I go to great lengths to prevent my voice from sharing a problem I would rather not discuss. And I know that Mom and Dad often play the same game, trying to protect me from problems I cannot solve for them. I appreciate their efforts.

My mother in particular. She has a very young voice on the phone. When she is feeling well physically, she could easily be mistaken for a woman of twenty. And I know that I have inherited this from her. When I listen to myself on the answering machine, I sometimes cannot reconcile what I hear with what I see of myself. I sound very much like my twenty-two-year-old daughter. And lately when I have called, my mother has sounded more perky. I know that's not how she is feeling because her physical ailments keep her in almost constant pain. But that's what she wants to project and I am grateful to her.

This past week, I met with a group of women to talk about the struggles of middle-aged children caring for aging parents. In a kind of resource roundtable, we shared things that have helped us and things that have hurt us. And one of the especially difficult topics that arose was the anguish of trying to carry out that responsibility long-distance.

When a frail and aging parent lives half a country away from a caretaking child, the telephone takes on a very special significance. Not only is it the mechanism for arranging for a visiting nurse, or the man to fix the roof, but it is the way we touch base with each other. And the pain that distance can cause becomes excruciating when a son or daughter reads need between the lines and cannot be there to respond. So the telephone is both a blessing and a curse.

And our ability to recognize unspoken messages, honed by years of living as children in the same home with our parents, seems to become more acute, if not more accurate.

We constantly receive such silent voice messages from friends and from spouses, from strangers who call and, in singsong monotony, interrupt our dinner as they try to sell us something. But the unspoken message in an aging parent's voice has a unique power. It's a kind of unsophisticated voice mail that requires no special line, no high-tech equipment. And in a mockery of all that electronic communications has become, our parents manage to push all the right buttons and leave all the necessary messages by simply speaking into the phone.

28

"You'll have to set aside a day to help us."

TIME-SHARING

I often think that time is like an accordion: sometimes it stretches and other times it contracts. And the sound that comes out, discordant or harmonious, depends upon the skill of the squeezer. My parents' closets sparked this image. Let me link the two for you.

Last week I joined my parents for dinner. They were very upset because in the course of routinely exterminating the nursing home, the staff had taken all of their things out of their drawers and closets and returned them in an unfamiliar order. For my parents, there is great security in predictability, order, and routine. This is not new for them. They have always been scheduled people. It's their nature. But as they have grown older, routine has taken on a special meaning. It feels safe to them. And any disruption feels threatening.

Mom's brow was furrowed with concern as she told me, "You'll have to set aside at least a day to help us straighten the closets." My first thought was, "That's ridiculous. The closets are tiny. I can do it in half an hour." But assuring them I would help, we finished eating and went to their room prepared for work.

It did take half an hour. I folded all their sweaters and underwear, replacing each piece in its long-familiar spot, exactly as I was instructed. All of Mom's slacks went on the left in her closet. All her blouses on the right. Her coat on the far right. I repeated the routine with Dad.

I could see them relax as order and predictability were restored. And then my mother put it into perspective for me. "It would have taken me three days to do this," she explained as she thanked me. Stopping to really listen to what she was saying, I was struck by the truth of her words. It would have taken them days to do what I had done so quickly. For both of them, standing for any period of time is trying and exhausting. Lifting multiple pieces of clothing is impossible. Instead of grabbing things in clumps as I had done, they would have had to organize and replace each item one at a time, stopping to rest in between. As I completed Dad's closet, he sighed. "I could never have stood there that long and done that."

Leaving them with a restored sense of peace, I thought about the visit as I drove home. I especially thought about my first reaction to their request for help. It had been to ridicule their prediction of the amount of time needed to reorganize their closets and drawers, and to be annoyed that they were asking me for a full day of my time. But from their point of view, they had been right. It would have taken *them* at least one full day to get the job done. And I realized that we each measure time in terms of our own capabilities. That's when I thought of the accordion.

And the image has stayed with me. So now when they ask for help with something, I try to remember that they are thinking of the job in terms of the time it would take for them to do it. Whether it's putting their names onto new clothing or straightening out books and newspapers in their room, my parents and I are seeing the same job through different lenses. Like using the opposite ends of a pair of binoculars to look at the same thing, what they see as enormous and looming, I often see as small and inconsequential.

But whether I think in terms of accordions or binoculars when I interact with my parents, what I have come to realize is that to understand them better, and to be more tolerant, I have to try to put myself in their place. And sometimes, as I look ahead at my own life, that's a little scary.

29

"I could no longer lift their wheelchairs into the car."

GUILT AND REALITY

The reality check came and I ignored it. I refused to recognize it . . . would not accept it . . . didn't want to think about it. I could no longer lift my mother's and father's wheelchairs into and out of my car. A part of me grieved and a part of me rejoiced. And the rest of me chewed on what that meant.

Hurt pride? Yes, that was part of it. I have always considered myself a physically strong woman. Strong enough to hoist baby carriages (the old-fashioned heavy kind) in and out of my car for years. Strong enough to move furniture with my husband. Strong enough to carry cartons of books from room to room. Strong enough to take my parents where they needed to go. Not anymore. Arthritis has put an end to that kind of lifting.

Guilt? Partly, yes. In addition to lifting the wheelchairs in and out of the car, there was the fetching and returning, the multiple trips to the room on the second floor of the nursing home. I felt guilty at the relief of giving up that responsibility.

Sad? Yes, absolutely. I was aging, my body was beginning to give me small messages with large implications. And sad also because my parents are more vulnerable now. They want company when they go to a doctor, support in case the news is frightening.

Frustrated? A great deal. I felt torn in two. Part of me wanted to be able to take them to doctors' appointments and another part didn't want the physical challenge; the pain in my back, the exhaustion that followed a four-hour sojourn in and out of my car to offices, rest rooms, and so forth.

And then, just as I was trying to digest all of these different feelings, my dad called to say that he was being scheduled for a CAT scan in two days to try and find out why he was falling so often and why he had become so dizzy. A crisis of conscience loomed. I had just come back from the orthopedist who told me my back discomfort was chronic but could be minimized by exercises. I was being scrupulously careful to follow all instructions for appropriate exercise. Lifting wheelchairs was not one of them.

Dad said he could go alone with the regular transport he has three days a week when he goes to dialysis. But then he called me later and asked me to go with him, and I could sense his fear. And so I thought of a compromise. He would take his scheduled transportation in a special van that accommodates wheelchairs, and I would meet him at the hospital to be with him through the scan. Then he could be transported home.

I think it's a compromise that will work for everyone. Even so, it leaves me sadly thoughtful. As my parents have become old and their need for physical help has grown, I have just begun to see myself as less able to meet some of their needs. They can't come to my home unless others are there to carry the wheelchairs up the front steps. They can't visit unless several people can help them walk the steps to my bathrooms. I can't do it on my own anymore.

And so reality confronts empathy, obligation, and guilt. Could be a toxic brew if I let it. That's why I find myself constantly searching for creative compromises. This time I was lucky. I came up with one. But I know more are coming. I've heard it said that necessity is the mother of invention. The challenge is to keep inventing solutions that keep that brew benign.

30

"I come out of work and see her slippers baking on the dashboard of my car."

FINDING WAYS TO HELP

If you go by my car in the parking lot near my office and see six pairs of pink fuzzy bedroom slippers resting on the dashboard, you will be witnessing the making of a memory.

There are very few things I can do to make life more pleasant for my mother. Her diabetes has left her incontinent and painfully fragile, though still remarkably feisty and alert. But one thing I *can* do to make her more comfortable is to wash her bedroom slippers weekly.

It took me a long time to find just the right slippers to satisfy her and meet the needs of her feet, made vulnerable by circulation problems. After several false starts and unproductive trips to three malls, I found just the right pair . . . and bought six of them. They didn't irritate her skin or rub the healing ulcer on her left foot. They had rubber soles but would still slide as she walked and had trouble lifting the foot that has suffered nerve damage. Best of all, they were washable.

And so we started our ritual. On the day that I visit, I gather the slippers of the week, place clean ones in the closet, then visit with Mom and Dad, reviewing the week's news and catching up on family gossip. Returning home, I toss the slippers into the washer and then the dryer. But they never seem to dry on the inside. Afraid of melting the rubber soles by turning up the heat, I began to look for ways to make sure the inside was dry when I returned them. I put the slippers next to the heating vent in my front hall. They took three days to dry inside. I put the slippers on a plastic table on my front porch that catches the morning sun. Still took three days, and if it rained I needed to start all over again.

I tried leaving them in various other places around the house, to no avail. They were always kind of in the way and out of place. Given the delicate condition of Mom's feet, this was no small concern. The slippers had to be clean and completely dry. Mildew and mold could cause trouble. But then I had the brilliant idea of putting them on my dashboard. In the sun all day. Protected from the weather. Ready and available to be delivered the moment they were dry. Not cluttering the front hall for days at a time. Now they dry quickly and conveniently. And I have had some funny moments explaining the pink fuzzy slippers to coworkers who need a lift somewhere.

Somehow, these slippers have become a visual symbol

and reminder of a value system that recognizes the importance of taking care of someone I love. They remind me to seek creative solutions to knotty problems, even trivial problems. But most of all, they remind me of Mom and the responsibility I accept in trying to help her. There is a certain sense of satisfaction I feel when I line the clean slippers up in the top of her closet, a sense perhaps of paying back.

Each time I come out of work and see her slippers baking on the dashboard of my car, I am glad I have found a way to make her more comfortable. And, as so often happens when I take the time to stop and think about how my parents are aging, I realize that someday I may be walking in her shoes instead of just washing them.

31

"I just got the most perfect gift!"

GETTING IT RIGHT

Over the years I have given gifts that have pleased the recipients and gifts that have kind of hung around and never been used. But the absolutely best gift I ever gave was one that cost me less than ten dollars, took about an hour to put together, and has given my mother contact with the people in the world whom she cares about and who care about her. I made her a telephone book for her birthday.

Within the past several years, although Mom has lost

much of both her vision and hearing, with modifications to her telephone, she can still enjoy the pleasure of making and receiving calls. One afternoon, when I was visiting, she asked me to read her the phone number of a friend and handed me the phone book she and my father had used for years. It was a ragtag pile of loose pages and small slips of paper, each precious because each contained the phone number of a brother, sister, friend, relative in New York, or medical/social service provider who had helped them maintain their independence over the years. Mom could no longer see well enough to read any of them.

As I held the jumble of pages in my hand, it occurred to me that this represented the skeleton of my parents' lives, the social structure around which they maintained themselves. I read Mom the number she needed and said I would try to fix their phone book.

On the drive home from the nursing home, I thought about my mother's needs. The phone numbers needed to be big enough for her to read, dark enough for her to see, and easy to find. An idea began to grow, and I headed for the nearest office supply store. Once there I purchased: one two-inch, three-ring white binder with a clear plastic sleeve on the front into which a sheet of paper could be inserted; one twenty-six-page set of tabbed dividers, each page having its own letter of the alphabet; one package of wide-lined, three-ring notebook paper; and one large felt-tipped chisel-point black marker.

I could hardly wait to begin the project. After dinner that evening, I spread the pages of my parents' phone book across my kitchen table and began. It was a trip through time that almost felt like an invasion of privacy. A good number of the people listed were no longer living, and culling the list was sad. But my enthusiasm grew as I began to see order emerging from chaos. I was making a tool.

Now each phone number got its own page. Using the black marker, I wrote each name and number in characters two inches high and then inserted the page (by last name) behind the appropriate alphabetical divider. All told, I must have written thirty or forty pages. Then I went to my computer. And in the largest and boldest font that would fit on a piece of notebook paper, I drew up a cover page that included the work and home numbers of all immediate family members, including the numbers of grandchildren living away at college. This page I slipped into the clear sleeve of the notebook so that it became the cover. Placing the unused paper at the back of the book for future additions, I wrapped my inspiration in birthday paper and counted the hours until I could take it to my mother.

Never have I enjoyed giving a gift as much as this one. Sitting on her bed as she opened it, I was gratified by the look on her face. Not one given easily to physical demonstrations of affection, she threw her arms around me, hugged me, and said, "Oh, I love it! I love it!" Just then, the phone rang. It was my mother's closest friend. "Helen," Mom began excitedly. "Judy just gave me the most perfect gift!"

I knew that I hadn't given her a telephone book. I had given her back her ability to connect with the world at her whim, on her own, whenever she wanted to. I had been able to return to her a small piece of the independence that age and failing vision had taken from her. It was the best gift I have ever given my mother.

32

"He was teaching me that I was important in his life."

THE LAST DANCE

I haven't danced with Dad in more than fifteen years. The memory swept over me unexpected and unbidden. I was watching TV, a late-night Saturday movie, and there was a scene of elegant men and women in period costumes pairing and sweeping in synchronized movement to the strains of the "Blue Danube Waltz."

I felt the lump in my throat swell as I remembered the evenings my father would return home from work, eat dinner quickly, and then succumb to my pleadings and give me a dance lesson. I was ten. He was thirty-eight. Now I'm fifty-three and Dad is eighty-one. A winding down of physical resources has made it very difficult for him to walk these days and his feet make him angry when they refuse to do his bidding.

But there had been a time when my father moved gracefully to the pattern I was now watching on the screen of my TV. And I found myself wondering, "How and why did he do it after a long day of work? Where did he find the energy?"

Never a particularly graceful man, my dad seemed to

feel clumsy with his body and played no sport that I can ever remember. But when he and my mother took to the dance floor, they moved together with an elegance and dignity that spoke little of the simple and very ordinary lives they led. It was a family joke that they could follow each other around the floor in perfect unison without ever touching.

And I remember how important and wonderful it made me feel when Dad twirled me around our tiny living room, teaching me to follow the pattern as he counted softly, "*One* two three. *One* two three." It's startling sometimes how a memory jumps into one's mind, surrounded by a halo of unexpected feelings.

For the past two years I have watched my father slowly lose his ability to walk, and become confined to a wheelchair for most of the day. I see my parents struggle to maintain their physical abilities and I get caught up in all kinds of efforts to help them . . . encouraging physical therapy . . . making sure their walkers have front wheels . . . making sure they have shoes that maximize their remaining abilities.

Wrapped up in their present needs, I see them as frail and failing. And then a late-night movie reminds me of who still lives inside the weathered exteriors I am looking at. This white-haired, bent-over, very senior citizen whose head now comes to just under my chin is the very same man who introduced me to the joyous abandon of a well-danced waltz.

It's been more than two weeks since I saw that movie, and the memory of dancing with my father has lingered in my mind. "When was the last time we danced?" I find myself wondering. And then I realize that since we never know when we will be doing something for the last time, what's important is to appreciate and enjoy as much as we can as often as we can.

But there is so much that passes between parents and their children. The moments of joy and the moments of pain stand out in our memories like beads strung along a fine thread. Every once in a while, an unexpected moment returns to mind, an ordinary day, an undocumented memory that has lain dormant for forty-three years. No black and white photographs recorded this moment. No one ever talked about those several evenings of dance lessons. And yet they are chiseled in my mind as if they had been carved in marble.

Now, belatedly, I have the special opportunity to savor the memory and share it with my dad. To tell him I didn't forget. To tell him his efforts went way beyond their intention. In addition to teaching me to dance, he was teaching me that I was important in his life when I was ten and he was thirty-eight. Hey, Dad, it works both ways.

33

"He was still giving his child his time."

RUNNING OUT OF TIME

I have a sampler on the wall of my family room that I have venerated for years. It says, "The best thing you can give a child is your time." But it's not complete. The best thing you can give *anyone* is your time. After much thought and agonizing, I gave my father five solid, unbroken hours of my time for Father's Day, and it was wonderful.

Needless to say, in the nursing home, space is at a premium: closets and drawers are full, wall space is limited. And as Father's Day approached I felt more and more frustrated about what I could give my dad that would be meaningful, useful, and small. I thought about what he needed, about what he wanted. At his age, I thought, wants are more important than needs. And then I remembered his scrapbook.

Two years ago my father, an inveterate scrapbook maker, had begun to collect articles on the building of the Holocaust Museum and about the fiftieth anniversary of the end of World War II. By the time he entered the nursing home, he could no longer manage using scissors, so the activities director invited two volunteer high school students to assist him with this project. Once a week for more than a year, they came on Thursdays to cut and paste at my father's direction. He would prepare for their visit a day in advance and at the appointed hour would have all the supplies spread across his bed. But then their school moved to a temporary building not convenient to the nursing home and their visits had to stop. The project remained in a box under my parents' television, temptingly unfinished, for almost a year.

This Father's Day, my son, who is working on a Ph.D. in American cultural history, and I went to visit Dad with scissors, glue, and tape to complete the project. We got there at

11 A.M. Dad had not been feeling well for the previous several weeks and almost seemed to be slowly withdrawing from an attachment to things beyond the limits of his room. We had to convince him to let us try to help with the scrapbook.

Despite his protesting, we laid it out on the bed. He began to think about it. We gathered the newspapers with articles that needed to be cut out. He began to look interested. We began clipping the stories. He began to give directions about what and how to cut. We began to have fun. He began to come alive.

Five hours later we were immersed in glue and gusto as Dad talked with Paul about his memories of the end of the war. We finally stopped at 4 P.M., by which time he had gotten too uncomfortable sitting in his wheelchair. He was a different man entirely from the one who had greeted us in the morning. Weary and in pain, he was also engaged, enthusiastic, and energized. And so were Paul and I.

The scrapbook was about two pages from completion when we left, carrying all the loose pages home in a box with the promise to return with a finished product. As the nurses were helping Dad into bed for a well-earned rest, we joked about being able to glue in the last few articles without Dad's instructions and oversight.

This weekend is the time Paul and I have set aside to finish the job. It's a true labor of love. When I told Dad I would bring it to him so he could keep it in his room, he replied, "I made it for you . . . to have a place in your home." And that's when I realized that unbeknownst to me, that sampler I had stitched about giving a child your time had become a symbol of my father's gift to me. Even with his very limited physical abilities, he was still giving his child his time.

34

"Not every happy moment has a reason we can understand."

RARE PLEASURE

I sat in the wheelchair feeling utterly at peace and totally surprised. I usually try to visit my parents on weekends. Often the visits are somewhat frantic as I try to carve out a solid piece of time that fits between their eating, napping, and various therapy schedules and my own agenda of weekend cleaning, shopping, and husband/wife nurturing.

But this evening was different. After a long and intense Thursday, and a poignant dinner out with an old friend who is also waging a kind of war with her mother's failing health, I decided to visit my parents because they needed some personal items that couldn't wait.

It was bitterly cold, and as I lugged the shopping bag into the elevator along with some laundry and dry cleaning items, I wondered what kind of day my parents had had and what kind of visit this would be.

As usual, their faces lit up when I knocked on their door and entered the room. They had both just showered and were in bed getting ready to go to sleep. I unpacked the goodies they had been waiting for and looked for a place to sit between them so that we could talk. The wheelchair looked best and I positioned myself between their two beds and we spent a few minutes catching up.

I fielded the usual review of problems they wanted help with and we just kind of chatted. They were both relaxed and reflective. I was wound up and exhausted. And then our banter began to have a kind of soothing effect upon me. I could feel myself relax as we talked about my three children and what each one was doing. And I realized that I spend much more mental time than I had been aware of worrying about my parents.

Seeing them scrubbed and relatively satisfied, and having the uninterrupted time to have a relaxed conversation with them calmed a spot in my mind that is normally always on alert and poised to respond to emergencies. I kind of "chair-walked" the wheelchair over to my dad's bed and talked a bit with him and then swung around and rolled closer to Mom, and we talked a bit. It felt very good to be able to do this.

Having this peaceful moment with my parents was special. I savored it as I sat watching my mom talk with her oldest friend on the telephone. Helen had called to say a quick hello. Mom laughed her old telephone laugh. The one I remember from my childhood when I had nothing better to do than to sit in the dining room and watch her talk on the phone.

And then I psychologically tucked my parents into bed as our conversation wound down and I prepared to leave. As is not too often the case, this visit had been a really satisfying one for all of us. I needed to see them in this calm and relaxed atmosphere. They needed to see me able to sit and not feeling pressured to jump and run. As I walked down the long corridor past all the other rooms in the nursing home, I felt unusually satisfied.

"Maybe they're more OK than I thought," I mused. The heavy weight that almost always is with me after a visit was missing. How and why was this time different? I wrestled with the question as I drove home . . . trying not to kill the good feeling with too much introspection. And the hint of an answer began to emerge. So often my parents and I meet on the run. Even on the weekends, their lives are carefully regimented and rigid, mostly by their own choice. And mine often feels like a series of pit stops between laps of a race. But this time all three of us had really been there, in the room, together, fully focused on each other, sharing the moment. It felt good.

I find I have this tendency to mentally revisit a knotty situation and pluck at the tangle until I feel it loosen. And I caught myself overthinking this happy moment in the same way, wondering if it would happen again. It wasn't knotty and it wasn't tangled. So what was I picking at? "Let it go," I counseled myself. "Savor it and let it go." Not every happy moment has a reason we can understand. Some just are.

35

"I get angry; I feel sad;
I am tired and usually very frightened."

DAD WON'T LISTEN

How do you help an aging parent who doesn't want help? Let me say at the outset that I haven't found an answer. I just keep hearing about people facing the same anguishing situations:

"My mother lives in Florida and is no longer safe living on her own. She refuses to allow anyone to come in to help her. I live in Maryland and I worry constantly."

"My father has become a menace on the road, but he won't let anyone else drive."

"My mom can't keep track of her finances anymore but she won't let me look at her checkbook."

Yes, there are counselors who offer help to people wrestling with these kinds of challenges. And I have no expertise in this kind of problem-solving. What I *do* know is how it feels to be confronted with a frail parent in denial, struggling to hold on the last vestiges of his or her independence and dignity.

For the past two years my father has found it increasingly difficult to walk. The residue of a stroke and the realities of a weakened body failed to convince him that it was time to use a walker regularly. And so he fell. Time and time again he fell. Before he and my mother moved into the nursing home, he fell in his apartment. Sometimes Mom called 911. Sometimes she called me. In the nursing home he has continued to fall despite being encouraged to call the nurses for help when he wants to walk. Something is driving him.

Understanding his need for independence, recognizing his pride or even vanity, knowing his stubbornness has not helped me. I have stood in the emergency room and watched a plastic surgeon sew twenty stitches in his face. I have accompanied him to CAT scans. I have explained the dangers of walking unaided. I have asked that if he wouldn't use a walker for himself, please use it for me. I have begged and pleaded. To no avail.

I think I know why he takes these risks. But understanding what motivates him doesn't help me at all as I am racing to the emergency room. I get angry. I feel sad. I am tired and usually very frightened. Is this the time he breaks his hip?

And so I have arrived at an intellectual procedure. I try to do what I can and accept the rest. Easy to say. Not easy to do. I have discussed the ramifications of a broken hip with Dad. His physician has advised him about using the walker. Physical therapists have worked with him, emphasizing safety and how to use assistive equipment. Nurses have encouraged him to call them for help. My mother harangues him endlessly. But when he sees a tissue lying on the floor, he still reaches forward to pick it up and tumbles out of his wheelchair. I know why he's reaching. It bothers him on the floor and he forgets he's old. There's a compulsive need to do what he wants that flies in the face of all reality.

Where does that leave me? Well, I have told myself that after I have done everything that I can to make him safe within the limits of what he will accept, I cannot hold myself responsible for what he chooses to do. That leaves him responsible and leaves me to deal with the consequences. That is the reality I face.

When frail and aging parents remain alert enough to make their own decisions, children find themselves torn between feelings of respect and responsibility. Respect for their independence and responsibility for their safety. And for those whose aging parents are losing their clarity, knowing when to step in is as agonizing as knowing what to do.

After speaking with friends, the only universal I have found in this situation is pain and that feeling of never knowing if we have done enough to let go of the responsibility we feel. Some days I can let go better than other days. But I know that now I will always share the consequences of my father's decisions. I've made that choice just as he's made his.

36

"I knew as soon as the words were out of my mouth that it was not the right thing to say."

BALANCING ACT

I knew as soon as the words were out of my mouth that it was not the right thing to say. It was a Thursday, and I had spent a very focused day at the office . . . the kind of day that leaves you feeling you have made a very small dent in a very large load.

Phoning my husband just before leaving my desk, I shared my plans for the remainder of the day. I could hear the fatigue and frustration in my own voice. "I'll visit Mom and Dad, come home . . . and probably go to bed."

After being married for almost thirty-two years, I can hear a great deal in my husband's voice. And his animation quickly turned to resignation. I knew what I was hearing. "Every time you visit your parents you come home drained," was the message in his sigh. "He is right," I thought. It's not my mom and dad's fault all the time. It's not my fault. It just happens, and he's tired of often having only half a wife.

My own children have commented on my preoccupation with my parents, which sometimes robs them of my complete attention. They have commented, but not complained. Like my husband, they recognize my struggle for balance. What often results is that all four of them periodically try to "read reality to me." They encourage me to let my concerns go for a while, to focus on something else, to enjoy our time together, to stay in the present moment and not worry about what is happening with Mom and Dad.

It's a delicate issue, and we often dance around each other with nonverbal messages that are earnestly sent and gratefully received. My husband will stand behind me as I wrestle with my parents' paperwork and, gently placing a hand on my shoulder, invite me to take a break for some coffee. My children, when they are home, will cook dinner after I have come from visiting my parents. I appreciate their unspoken understanding more than I can tell them.

But yesterday, when I heard myself complaining, a light-bulb went on. "This is not fair to my family," I thought. "Coming home and going to bed is not handling the issue. It's hiding from it. You have choices," I lectured myself. And so I resolved to do better than that.

I *did* visit Mom and Dad, and it *was* difficult. Neither of them is feeling very well, and untangling the issues that are medical from those that are mental is hard. Are they depressed or ill? It was a brief visit because I decided I needed to speak with their physicians. And so I left quickly to make the phone call from my home. Stopping at the store on the way home, I bought something special for dinner and stocked up on goodies that would make the next several dinners nice instead of just necessary.

Arriving home, I called the doctors, spoke with both of them, and felt that I had been both heard and supported. Then I began dinner. My daughter came home with news of her day and it was fun talking. And then my husband drove into the driveway. Watching him emerge from the car, I started to laugh the chuckle of long-married appreciation.

The resignation I had heard in his voice on the phone that afternoon had been translated into action. He had *also* stopped at the store, thinking I would be too exhausted to prepare dinner. We now have four half-gallons of milk in the refrigerator, three of orange juice, six bottles of diet soda, more ears of corn than I can count, packages of imitation crab, and several chicken pot pie dinners, not to mention a butter pound cake and a cherry pie.

It was good to laugh together as we tried to fit his purchases and mine into an already overstuffed refrigerator. I was moved by his understanding and the unspoken message in his shopping. The three of us went upstairs to change clothes and ended up sitting on our bed joking about how it feels to have our new college graduate back in the family nest. Then the phone rang. It was the nursing home. My father had fallen again, and taken his wheelchair along with him. A tooth was chipped and his lip was slightly cut, but he was OK. I didn't need to come.

Silently, as I talked with the nurse on the phone, my husband and daughter left the bedroom. I could feel the animation draining out of our evening. Not this time, I promised myself. And when I was assured that Dad was OK, I very consciously tried to redirect my thoughts as well as my actions. Dinner ended up being both good and fun. The teasing that had evaporated with the phone call was back at the dinner table. And as I listened to my husband and daughter plow through a lively discussion about feminism and how times have changed, I reminded myself that I really do have choices. The hard part is getting myself to make good ones.

37

"Pick up her foot and let me see that shoe."

SHOWING LOVE

What makes some ordinary moments extraordinary? So special that you know you will remember them forever? I had one with my parents last night and I have been thinking about it ever since. My dad made a very simple gesture, one hardly worth remembering. But I think it was pregnant with such meaning that my mind took a mental snapshot without my even pushing the button. Dad checked the fit of my mother's new shoes.

From the time I can remember, Dad has been checking the fit of shoes: on children, on old people, on teenagers. And often, on weekends when we were in high school and college, my brother and I worked alongside him at one of his stores, manning the cash register or fitting shoes ourselves.

He did this for more than thirty years. At the age of sixty-two my father retired to read, study art, collect books, listen to classical music, and lecture at the National Portrait Gallery as a docent. And over the years, as health problems arose, I forgot who he used to be and concentrated on who he had become. He is my father struggling with a kidney problem, a gall bladder problem, a heart problem, a collapsed lung problem. And many of our interactions revolve around his health issues.

That's why last night was such a jolt. After work I stopped by for a visit. It was Friday night, and they had already had dinner. And as they both sat in their wheelchairs in a room crowded with assistive equipment, we had a very personal discussion about family relationships and what my parents wished to see happen before they die. My mother initiated the conversation, which was very unusual for her.

Maybe it was because we were being so honest with each

other that my mind was particularly attuned to feelings. I don't know. But as the conversation wound down and we were decelerating the emotional content of what we had been talking about, I noticed that my mother was wearing new shoes. I knew that my brother had taken her to get them months ago and that they had to be specially ordered. And I knew that it meant a great deal to her to have them. Mom has always been particular about the clunky orthopedic shoes her poor circulation required her to wear, keeping them sparkling white, gleamingly polished. Over the past two years, though, her shoes had aged even more quickly than she.

So I recognized that finally having her new shoes was a big deal and I complimented her on how they looked. When I did, my father said, "Wheel Mom over to me." Not understanding why, I did as he asked. "Now, pick up her foot and let me see that shoe." Again, I did as he asked. And then, very slowly, my father reached over and checked the fit of my mother's shoes.

As a diabetic with neuropathy, my mother has no feeling in her hands and feet. Any rubbing in her shoe can cause an ulcer and possibly lead to gangrene. So standing there in the fading light of day I watched my father reach slowly across the distance between their two wheelchairs. His hand is old and weathered. His wedding ring slides up and down between palm and knuckle. But with great assurance, he checked the width of the shoe, and the length of the shoe, where my mother's toes reached. He looked for signs of the leather pulling or being stretched. And he declared it a good fit.

A very ordinary moment, hardly worth remembering, I would have thought. But it symbolized the years of my father's work life. It symbolized the expertise he had developed. It symbolized his caring for and about my mother. And it was over in seconds. But I have it now forever. How many times does this happen to simple people, plain families living ordinary lives? We can't plan these moments. They just occur and we just remember. For me, they seem to be moments that link the past with the present in a poignant way. They are bridges to understanding.

38

"My father and I have rarely discussed love."

FAMILY ALBUMS: BURIED TREASURE

It's 1 A.M. on a Wednesday morning and the box is keeping me awake. This evening my husband and I rooted around in our jumbled garage and took it from its resting place. Like buried treasure, it had lain hidden for the more than two years since my parents dismantled their home.

In its brown paper depths I found my father's four white photograph albums containing everything he was ever proud of, everything he loves. Neatly laid out in eye-catching design were pages of photographs of my brother and his family, my family, other relatives, friends, letters, birth announcements, postcards, newspaper articles about family accomplishments, my father's junior high school diploma, poems Dad wrote to Mom on her birthday. Page after page of pride Dad has never been comfortable enough to articulate.

When my parents moved into the nursing home they discarded many things. But my father's extensive book collection, his lifelong pride and joy, was carefully packed for storage in my garage. Neither he nor I could part with a single book. And buried among the books about history, art, philosophy, and science were these four books about love.

A request for some old family photographs had launched me on this search through the pile of cartons neatly stacked in my garage. Although I had seen the albums many times over the years, and had even on occasion leafed through them, I had never felt the full impact of their message until tonight. Maybe it's because Dad has not been well lately and I am thinking about losing him. Maybe it's because I have been angry lately and frustrated by increasing responsibilities for my parents' growing needs. Maybe it's because I'm planning a vacation that will take me hundreds of miles away at a time when both Mom and Dad seem so very weak.

But as I lingered over each page, seeing both my parents and my extended family when we were all so much younger, I was tremendously moved by what this effort represented. By the time I got to the final album I had watched all of my cousins move from infancy into adulthood and careers. I had seen all of my children graduate from all of their schools. I had watched my father lose one after another of his sisters. I had reviewed my engagement, marriage, motherhood, and budding writing career. I had watched my brother negotiate the road from young family hippiedom to middle-aged executive. And in countless photographs, I had seen my husband and me age together on my parents' couch, moving from young love and new marriage through young children and new responsibilities into middle age and midlife challenges.

And although my father can talk endlessly about modern art and inquire ceaselessly into new scientific findings, we have rarely discussed love. Perhaps for his gender, in his generation, love is a given, silent and unspoken. Then again, it may be that his personality prohibits its easy expression.

But today, through these albums, in graphic and unambiguous terms, he made the message clear. And I am so very grateful that he is here so that I can tell him I got it. When I visit I'll bring the albums with me so we can look at them together. There is something very satisfying about acknowledging love. It balances the anger, frustration, sadness, guilt, and fear that have been my companions on this journey with my parents into their old age. Like shock absorbers, love smoothes out the ride if not the road.

PART III

Night

Death

The night is dark for a reason. We are forced to focus on what we think and feel when we cannot see. Darkness blots out all other distractions and we must find our way through unknown passages, relying on our instincts. So too with death.

It is a lonely and frightening journey; a place without candles. It is where we go in trust, in belief, in faith. Some go in hope, others in despair. Some willingly, others raging against the darkness. And then there are those who go because their children make the choice to send them there.

It is my decision to remove my parents from life support in accordance with their wishes. I have the durable power of attorney for health care, and we have discussed this decision many times as a family. All of their many doctors concur. That does not ease the searing pain of making it happen. "I must not turn away from this," I tell myself. "I must face it and be their companion. This is the final mile and we must walk it together as planned." Within eight weeks of each other, they die.

Despite our less than perfect past relationships, my parents and I have come to this place together, working hard at the end to help and appreciate each other. And although my love for them has felt protective, I recognize now that they love and are protecting me as well by participating in this final planning process. It is a gift we give each other.

39

"Dad, are you afraid to die?
Would you talk with me about your feelings?"

THE GIFT OF CONVERSATION

Most parents say that they would do almost anything to protect their children from pain. Five minutes before they are born, we don't know them at all and five minutes later, we would give our lives for them. Starting from birth and the time that we "kiss the boo-boo" and watch the tears magically evaporate from those chubby cheeks, until the day we draw our last breath, we move heaven and earth to prevent needless suffering in our children.

But so often we hold back, we hesitate, we delay doing one thing that in the end can prove to be the most profoundly generous gift we can ever give to our children. We don't help ease the agony of one of the most painful things that they may ever experience. Aging parents and adult children need to learn to talk with one another more openly about dying, to speak about pain, death, and the risks as well as the benefits of medical technology.

My parents were probably two of the most inarticulate people I have ever known when it came to expressing their caring. That kind of sensitivity eluded them. Life often frightened them. But death didn't. And the gift they gave my brother and me in the last year of their lives was to be willing to talk about the approaching end openly, honestly, and as frequently as was necessary.

Both parties must be willing to enter and explore this frightening new territory. Many years ago, after my father had had bypass surgery, he had a conversation about his own death with a cousin of mine. She asked him if he had expressed his feelings to me. "No," he replied. "I'm afraid it might frighten Judy." My cousin was wise enough and kind enough to tell me about her conversation with my father. And from that moment, I resolved to try and let my father know that I was not afraid to talk with him about his death.

It wasn't easy. And at times it almost seemed like wildly humorous black comedy. My father had so many surgeries in the last twenty years of his life that we joked about putting in zippers. And when he was more robust, in his sixties and seventies, we didn't speak much about death because the assumption was always that he would recover. I see now that that was a mistake. And I now think that as adults, we should let the people we love and those who love us know how we feel about our own deaths and how we wish to approach life and death decisions for medical treatment.

It wasn't until my father was eighty that our dialogue began in earnest. Usually the conversations happened when we were facing some medical condition together. I became bolder about asking him questions, initiating the delicate topic of death to let him know that I wasn't afraid, that he wouldn't hurt me by talking about it. And one day, as he was revisiting his life experiences with me while we waited for a medical appointment, I found the right moment and asked him, "Dad, are you afraid to die? Would you talk with me about your feelings?"

It was the first olive out of the jar. He began to speak, telling me how he felt and what he wanted. I promised that I would care for Mom if he died first. It was open, emotional, and, I think, cathartic for both of us. And it was only the first of many conversations.

Months later, as he grew weaker and my brother and I felt he might soon die, we set aside a Sunday and visited him and my mother. Both my brother and I had spoken with Dad about this subject before, but privately, never together and never in the presence of my mother. We wanted clarity with both of them, but had planned to speak with them one at a time. Talking quietly so that my mother, who was asleep (and hard of hearing), could not listen, we talked with Dad about his advance directive, about resuscitation, about his death.

And then, out of the blue, in her typically blunt and honest way, my mother, who we thought had been asleep, said, "Do you want to know what I think about dying?" Stunned, we turned to her bed and began a four-way dialogue that was to represent my parents' greatest gift to their children.

Despite a clear advance directive detailing their wishes for treatment or removal of treatment if they became critically ill, and despite their conversations with their doctors, in the end, it became my brother's and my responsibility to make the final life and death decisions on their behalf. And by the grace of God and the courage of my parents, we both felt that we knew what they wanted and understood their beliefs about life after death, and we felt clearly and cleanly anointed as their advocates.

We spoke openly and at length with all of their caregivers. And when the time of dying came for each of my parents—amid all the chaos of the intensive care units, the doctors, nurses—my brother and I followed a logical extension of their wishes and removed them from life support, not without great pain and much sorrow, but with a clear conscience. Those conversations were and continue to be my parents' greatest gift to us.

40

"If you want to talk about dying, I'm ready to listen."

PREPARING TOGETHER

The tape reeled slowly out of the electrocardiograph machine as my father lay on the examining table. The squiggly lines meant nothing to me. My father was being evaluated for the surgical repair of his dialysis graft. And I was preparing for some repair work myself.

I began slowly and thoughtfully, selecting my words one at a time. I had spent the entire week thinking about how to correct my mistake. "You know, Dad, last week when you were giving me such detailed instructions about how you wanted your scrapbook on the Holocaust Museum finished,

I joked with you about whether or not you were trying to tell me something. And I told you that you couldn't possibly die because you had to finish the book. I remember we both smiled." Dad nodded.

"Well, I just want to tell you that I understand that dying is no joking matter and if you were telling me that you want to talk about it, I'm ready to listen." I sensed that my father and I were fully focused on each other and on the previously taboo subject I had raised. So I continued. "I'm not afraid to talk about death. I think you were asking to talk about it when you were explaining what you wanted done with the scrapbook. And somehow, I think I missed your message then, but I get it now." Dad nodded again.

"Are you scared?" I asked, opening the door further. Dad cleared his throat and looked directly at me. We were alone in the examining room. "No," he answered in a surprisingly strong voice. "Why not?" I was curious. And thus my father and I were launched into a discussion of his death and his feelings about it.

"Because when I went into cardiac arrest two years ago, I wasn't aware of any discomfort. I didn't feel any pain. I had no knowledge of what was happening to me. I wasn't frightened. It just happened . . . that quickly. So if that's what death is like, I'm not afraid." "Do you think about it?" I asked. "Sure," he responded. "Well, I got the sense," I continued, "that you might want to talk. And I want you to know that I'm open to any discussion you want to have with me about death."

The word hung in the air between us, and again, my father's direct gaze told me I was on the right track. "I appreciate that," my father said, as the nurse returned to the room to unhook him from the machine. The moment of privacy and intense intimacy had passed, but the look in my father's eyes told me that I had not been mistaken in opening that door. His thoughts and feelings would no longer have to be indirect, or his messages in coded phrases. We could now speak directly about this subject if he wanted.

"Den and I will always take care of Mom," I said, because I know he worries about her whenever he leaves their room to go to the hospital for dialysis. And for the first time in our conversation, I had to swallow an enormous lump in my throat. He looked at me once more and nodded silently.

I let the moment go and felt the tension ease as my body relaxed. It was done. I had repaired the damage. And I was grateful to Elisabeth Kübler-Ross, whose books on death and dying I had just begun to explore. Her careful, commonsense suggestions about whether or how to broach this subject with an ill and aging loved one had been helpful guideposts as I groped in the darkness of my own fear, denial, and ignorance.

Raising the issue of death with my father also forced me to confront my own mortality. And I think that this is healthy, though sometimes very painful, growth for me. I had the sense that it was helpful and good for my father as well. He told me he was glad we had talked.

And while the nurse peeled the plastic circles from my father's chest as she unhooked him from the machine, I looked at his flaccid arms and remembered them as they had been when I was a child. He used to make the bulging muscles dance to a silly song he sang: "All the girls in France do the hootchie kootchie dance. . . ." He could make them alternately jump to the rhythm of the song. His arms are very different now. We are all going in that direction, I thought, as I helped my father dress to leave the doctor's office. But we don't have to go alone.

41

"The decision was made to insert a chest tube."

MEDICAL EMERGENCIES

We were at war again and death was losing this time. As I looked along the bays in the emergency room at Holy Cross Hospital, I recognized many that I had already visited while accompanying my parents through various unexpected medical situations. I saw the one Dad used when he went into cardiac arrest, and another Mom used when she fell and broke several ribs. There was the diabetic reaction one and the urinary-tract infection one. Memories flooded back, but this visit was to be very different.

The call from the dialysis unit had come into my office at closing time. "Your dad is very lethargic and not alert. We're sending him to the emergency room immediately." Fifteen minutes later I was at his side, relieved to see he recognized me and was speaking clearly. But he was breathing in painfully short pants.

The pulmonary specialist worked on my father, explaining that he was going to try to withdraw the fluid surrounding my father's left lung with a syringe. I had seen this done to Dad before. But this time it didn't work. The decision was then made to insert a chest tube to drain the fluid. It was critical to relieve the pressure on his lung immediately and the procedure had to be done right there in the emergency room.

But instead of sending me to the waiting room, the surgeon asked me to help him by holding my father in the necessary position as he and the nurse worked to put the tube in place. And so with my arms around Dad to help him stay in place, I watched the nurse wheel in a cart of instruments as the surgeon injected a local anesthetic. Selecting a scalpel, the surgeon drew a two-inch dash between the ribs on my father's left side. Probing for an opening between them with his finger, he inserted a clear plastic tube that immediately filled with an amber-colored fluid. Attaching the tube to a bubbling suction device, he began sewing the tube in place, explaining to me that it would have to remain as a drain for several days. I watched him wind and tie the black silk sutures that would anchor the tube, and marveled at the dexterity required to stitch and sew a human being.

I talked with Dad during the procedure. He was once again stoic about his weakening body. His hand stayed in mine, warm to the touch and solid. I was grateful to both give and receive reassurance through this physical contact. And in the hours following surgery, Dad and I began to talk about many painful things . . . the what-he-would-want-done-ifs. But a nurse wisely drew me aside to remind me that Dad had been given a sedative and that this was perhaps not the best time to assess his priorities. She was right, of course. And I promised myself to talk with Dad about this at a better time.

All this happened three days ago, but an unusual feeling has stayed with me. When I was holding Dad as the doctor and nurse worked to save his life, I felt a special closeness to all of them. We were a team and we were waging a war. It was an intimate moment I will never forget. For the first time, I wasn't sitting in the waiting room feeling helpless and afraid. I was holding Dad and helping the staff. But they were also helping me. When I left the hospital at 1 A.M., I walked through the dark parking lot with feelings of profound respect: for my father, who is strong; for the nurse and doctor, who are skilled; and for myself, because I had stayed calm, been helpful, and learned that I could live through this.

42

"Sometimes my life seems to be one continuous exercise in triage."

THE COST OF CARE

There is a tiredness beyond defining that comes with responsibility for the care and comfort of aging parents. It's a strange exhaustion because it doesn't always build. Rather, it pops in and out of my life with no advance notice, sapping time and energy in ways I had not planned for but must plan around.

Today, for instance. I just returned from a grueling four-day national conference of twelve-hour workdays and had planned to spend the day catching up on my writing. But the pile of insurance statements and paper minutiae involving my parents has grown enormous, and I need to gather some of this together to send to my brother, who processes the medical parts and sends instructions back to me about what he has done and what I need to do.

This morning I phoned my father's doctor with some questions about Dad's condition and needed to be available to receive his reply. After speaking with the doctor, there were unresolved issues with the nursing home that needed to be addressed. So I phoned the nursing home administrator and am now awaiting her call.

Meanwhile I must pay the few monthly bills that my parents still incur, even though they are on Medicaid. And I have to make time to purchase several items they have asked for. Their checking accounts (required by Medicaid to be separate) need balancing. And I also just got a phone call from a concerned relative who said that my dad seemed to be very weak when she visited him while I was out of town. So I'm dealing with the tug to run over to visit even though I have scheduled work for the rest of the day and well into the evening.

Sometimes my life seems to be one continuous exercise in triage. At least when you go to the emergency room there is someone who immediately assesses your level of need and makes a decision about what to attend to first. Maybe that's what I need at home—someone who can tell me what to do and in which order. I know, of course, that this is foolish thinking. But deciding, on a daily basis, which of my responsibilities to my parents need handling, and in what order, drains some major voltage from my battery. Sometimes it's not even the doing that is draining . . . it's the deciding.

And then there are those times when I reach for that extra surge of energy to meet a crisis or handle a specific frustration. Unlike the electrical surges that trip a circuit breaker when the line is overloaded, the surges that invade my life as a caregiver do not always immediately blow a fuse. Often that comes later, after I have met the need or handled the emergency. Sometimes I can't even connect the event with the surge. Then it is particularly hard, because the weariness seems to come from nowhere, and I have to work hard to think back and link the cause to the effect.

Today I did some mental sleuthing because my tiredness felt overwhelming. My father had become gravely ill just the week before I was scheduled to attend my professional association's conference in Pittsburgh. As membership director, I had spent considerable time planning for this yearly event. To go or not to go . . . that was the question. The four doctors treating my father gave me their best prognosis. It was guarded. He was improving. No one had a crystal ball and the future remained unclear. So using my best gut-guessing techniques, I decided to attend the conference and fly home if it became necessary. It was, thankfully, unnecessary and my father continues to remain stable though weakened.

But I realized that I am paying for that intense expense of decision-making energy with the generalized sadness and exhaustion that I feel today. Fly now pay later may be good for the consumer, but not for the caregiver. At least for today, I have been able to figure out which trip I am paying for.

43

"Three of us had fathers who were gravely ill."

THE SEESAW

It's hard to feel any real balance in your life when a parent is critically ill. Try as you might to focus on work and family responsibilities, there is an irresistible pull that draws you into caregiving, decision making, and awkward and often ill-timed efforts to give support or come to closure. Many of us reach this point with a great deal left that we want or need to say to a parent. We often arrive unexpectedly at these possibly final moments carrying lots of baggage.

It was a poignant and difficult week at my office. Three of the seven of us had fathers who were gravely ill. Meetings were interrupted by phone calls from doctors, hospitals, and family members. The phrases "heart attack," "bone cancer," and "collapsed lung" bounced around the cubicles of our offices just audibly enough to cause everyone else to look up inquiringly. The silent touch of a colleague's hand on the shoulder spoke volumes as we tried to support and comfort each other.

And then there were those moments when we had to talk . . . about the illnesses, about our fears, about our relationships with our fathers. And in the telling, we fleshed each other out, became more than the receptionist, the accountant, the editor. All at once, we were the son, the daughter, the brother, the sister. We were more whole to each other. We allowed ourselves, in our need, to be more vulnerable.

And then, there also was the relief of work, the distraction offered by office responsibilities and routine, the focus on the present, drawing us away from intense worry about our fathers and families and futures. And sometimes, at least for me, there was a bit of guilt at feeling such relief.

At week's end, we left the office in limbo. One father was improving and two were still in critical condition. And today, when we returned to work, one had died. It was not my father. But watching my colleague and listening to his anguish, I almost felt as if I were practicing for the pain. I tried to say things I thought might help. I reminded myself to relish each day with my parents, with my family, and with myself. And I realized that when a parent dies, regardless of the quality of your relationship, the balance in your life is never quite the same.

And so my colleagues and I straddle the fulcrum, shifting our weight and roles as the times demand; one moment we are workers, another we are sons or daughters, and still another we are parents, lovers, and friends. Everyone does this. It's just that this week, the three of us in my office spent a great deal of time focused on being the children of our fragile fathers. And that made it very, very hard to keep the seesaw level.

44

"She's having difficulty breathing."

APPROACHING DEATH

I never thought Mom would go first. Dad was always sicker. The call from a coworker came while I was attending a seminar in downtown Washington. "Judy, your mom's being taken to the hospital. She's having difficulty breathing." It was a long Metro ride back to my car . . . time to think . . . time to prepare . . . time to cry.

Just three days before, my brother and I had had a discussion with both of my parents about their wishes regarding resuscitation in the event that either went into cardiac arrest. As the Metro jerked and twisted through dark tunnels, I recalled the discussion in vivid detail. The tears came and I let them.

We are ready, I thought. Both my parents have advance directives outlining their wishes about the quality of their lives and what they want done in a life-threatening medical emergency. I have durable power of attorney for health care and am the one designated to see that these wishes are followed. We have had many discussions about exactly what they want. I have read the directives to my parents, and they have initialed each page.

Although the documents are very detailed and specific about such issues as resuscitation, tube feeding, and the like, they still make me the bottom line on implementation. So my brother and I had set aside last Sunday morning to talk with my parents about whether or not they wanted to be "coded,"—that is, whether or not they would want to be resuscitated if their hearts stopped beating. We explained that that might mean authorizing medical personnel to do CPR on them and to possibly place them on a respirator.

It was an intense morning as my brother and I asked our mother and our father individually what their wishes were. We explored all the options we could think of, shared all the information we knew, and discussed our feelings. In the end, my father opted for what is known as a "no code." That means that should his heart stop beating, he would want us to let him die. He was philosophical and even eloquent in the discussion. "My life has been worthwhile," he told us, "and you children have been the diamonds in my life. It's time," he whispered. My brother knelt next to Dad's bed and I stood with my arm around my brother's shoulder. We cried together and thanked Dad for helping us be clear about what he wanted and what we might have to authorize.

Then we turned to Mom. For a while now my mother has been depressed because of her worsening diabetes and all the resulting disabilities. She has talked about death often, almost in a welcoming way. But when we put the question to her directly, "Mom, if you were to go into cardiac arrest, would you want to be resuscitated?" she surprised us. After several moments of quiet thought, she nodded yes. To be sure we understood her wishes, I repeated what I understood. And with a very direct look, she said, "Yes."

All these thoughts came flooding back as I rode the train into Silver Spring. The car ride to the hospital seemed to take forever. In the emergency room, I found my mother weakened and on oxygen. Very quickly, her condition worsened as she aspirated fluid into her lungs. The hospital had a copy of her advance directive. And as her agent, I was asked to give permission for the doctors to put her on a respirator. Here I was, two days after our discussion, having to implement her wishes, make medical decisions on her behalf.

Although this was not yet cardiac arrest, I knew she wanted to live. I knew her life still had sufficient quality for her. And I knew what to do if that quality diminished. I was very grateful to my parents for being clear about their wishes. *They* had made the decision and I was their instrument. No guilt. No doubt.

The crises worsened: internal bleeding, pneumonia, coma. But through it all, I felt I had been given direction by my mother. Each time I spoke with a doctor or made decisions with the medical staff of the intensive care unit, I felt comfortable with the treatment she was receiving. My mother's physicians have been supportive, informative, and also appreciative of the directions I could clearly give them about my mother's wishes.

Today my mother awoke from a four-day coma. Today they were able to take her off the respirator. Today she was able to respond to my questions with looks and nods and squeezes of my hand. Today, my mother is alive—very ill, but alive. And each time I leave the intensive care unit of the hospital and walk slowly out into the everyday world, I silently thank my parents for the guilt, doubt, and pain they have spared me by addressing these life-and-death decisions beforehand. And when I cry, there is relief mixed with the sadness. It is worth the pain of having a "code, no code" discussion to be spared the agony of wondering if you've made the right decision, the decision your parents would have wanted. My mother told me what she wanted. I can live with her decision and those I may have yet to make for her. My father is also gravely ill. More choices are coming. I think I am ready.

45

"I have scoured my soul
and decided to let my mother die."

ALLOWING DEATH: THE ADVANCE DIRECTIVE

For the past two weeks my mother has drifted toward and then away from and then back toward death. Doctors, nurses, and my family have fought hand-to-hand combat with the Grim Reaper, and I found myself alternately exhorting my mother to come back and to let go.

I have cried and stood endlessly by her bed and had long and agonizing discussions with my brother, her doctors, my husband and children. I have exhausted my mind with pros and cons, read and reread my mother's advance directive, and recalled countless conversations with my mother about death. I have scoured my soul. And I have decided to let my mother die.

For all my textbook preparation for this moment, I find myself swept by waves of apprehension. Not for Mom. She is suffering in ways she would never want to prolong. The vast majority of the many medical specialists attending her have advised us that her suffering will probably continue. In my heart of hearts I know that my mother would not want to live under the conditions of the past two weeks: the feeding tube, the recurrent pneumonia, the repeated suctioning of her lungs, the inability to swallow, the incontinence, the impaired intellect.

The apprehension I feel is for myself. And the question I wrestle with is whether I will be able to live comfortably with this decision to remove her from life support. I think that I will. I hope that I will. I pray that I will. In her advance directive my mother authorized my brother and me to stop all heroic life support efforts when "the burdens of continuing to live become greater than the benefits" for her. If I were to sit down with a piece of paper folded down the middle, as I usually do when considering the big decisions of life, and list the pros and cons of keeping my mother alive, the list would be enormously lopsided. And in my past experience, such a list has always made decisions easier. The powerful surge of preparation has peaked with the completion of the list and is usually followed by a calm feeling of surety that has allowed me to make a decision and move on with my life. And in my mind, endlessly over the past two weeks, I have gone over the list of reasons to allow my mother to die. I can't find the calm. I can't find the peace. But I can feel the pain.

My mother has said she is not afraid to die. She has told me what she thinks will happen to her when she dies, and I hope what she thinks and believes is true. And although we have also discussed her decision to be resuscitated if she should go into cardiac arrest, it was always with the understanding that she would hopefully be returned to her full intellect and that the status quo of her health would continue. My father has approached death more times than I can count and has returned weakened, but intellectually intact. She was hoping for the same.

But life doesn't always happen as we hope. In the beginning of this siege, as she drifted in and out of awareness, my mother's doctor asked her if she "wanted to make it." In a moment of clarity, she nodded yes. We took that as a mandate and launched a war to return her body to as close to its previous level of function as possible. However, she began to lose things: her ability to breathe unaided, her ability to swallow, her ability to respond to commands. And we began to lose her in our minds, to imagine what life would be like without her, what *her* life would be like under what her doctors caution will be continuing and recurrent conditions.

Each family member has had an opportunity to share opinions and feelings. This morning, Sunday, my brother and his family will come to breakfast at my home and we will share a final moment of discussion before heading to the nursing home for advice from my father. Dad, who is gravely ill himself, reminded me last night that "Mom doesn't want any elaborate efforts made" to keep her alive. But he also cautioned that we not make the decision too quickly. How long is too long? I spend the night agonizing over this.

Today I awoke knowing that I would go to the hospital and tell the doctors and nurses what my mother has authorized us to do on her behalf. They have been asking, and I have been concurring, to surgically put in tubes to sustain my mother, to put her on a respirator, to do whatever it takes to keep her alive. Now, after all the discussions, after rereading her directive, after all the advice, my brother and I have decided to reverse the process and allow her "to meet her Maker," as her physician gently put it in his discussion with us.

I need to take a moment to thank these people who have waged war alongside my mother: the doctors and nurses, the respiratory specialists, the speech pathologists, the phlebotomists. Not only for their expertise, skill, and opinions, but for their compassion, candor, and help in bringing us to this decision.

I think there is no lonelier decision to make in this world than the one to allow a parent (or any loved one) to die. I pray with all my heart to spare my children this agony. I will talk with them about my wishes and will write an advance directive for myself soon. But not just now. I have promised myself to feel, and to let my husband and children see and share, the pain of this decision. It is mine to make and mine to live with. But their love, comfort, and support have made this moment bearable. And I hope that on the other side of this decision, both my mother and I will find peace.

46

"What would be the purpose of continuing treatment and testing?"

IMPLEMENTING DEATH

Mom's nurse found my brother and me standing in the busy hallway outside of her hospital room trying to finalize the wrenching decision to allow Mom to die. She had cared for my mother since she was moved out of intensive care after a two-week battle with life-threatening emergencies. And we were discovering that there is a huge difference between deciding to do something and actually doing it. Discussions at my kitchen table had seemed softer, more abstract and loving than decisions made in a hospital hallway. My brother and I were struggling to talk intimately in the crowded corridor as the nurse approached.

Very gently, she touched our shoulders and invited us into a small quiet room down the hall that had a door we could close for the privacy the moment cried out for. She asked if she could join us and, in an extraordinary act of compassion and courage, offered to help us in any way she could.

Over the next hour, as we tried to evaluate the burdens and benefits to Mom of continuing treatment, this extraordinary nurse helped us untangle the options and face honestly the choices we had. Mom's primary physician had reluctantly suggested one more test and he needed our consent. My brother and I had a question about the test but we were hesitant to try and reach him at his office. The nurse placed the call, explained our need, and handed us the phone. He answered our question.

Again the three of us spoke intensely. Another question arose. Again Mom's nurse phoned the physician and explained that we had another question. The physician came to the phone, and again we had the information we needed. She did not do this for us. Rather, she helped us do this for ourselves.

Mom's prognosis was not good and she was not alert. We had called in a sixth specialist whose opinion about her condition left us in even greater agony. Contrary to the other physicians treating her, who warned that her problems would more than likely continue or recur, necessitating a return to the respirator and the probability of additional damage, he felt she could still recover enough to have a limited but meaningful quality of life. Our problem was that from prior discussions with Mom and a careful reading of her advance directive, we knew that what he was describing as meaningful was not what she wanted. And my brother and I felt torn between wanting her to live and fearing that the continued suffering was not what she would choose.

Finally, after facilitating our phone calls to the doctor, after listening to our talking and grieving and crying and raging, the nurse asked quietly, "What would be the purpose of continuing treatment and testing?" It was not a statement. It was a question. It was the right question.

My brother and I made the decision, as we believed Mom would have wished, to stop everything. No more tests, no tubes, no needles, no suctioning. We sat together on the couches in the small quiet room and the three of us cried as we acknowledged the difficulty of what we had just been through and would now face.

The nurse left us to comfort each other in privacy, and ten minutes later when we emerged from the room, she had already removed all the tubes and needles. Mom was resting comfortably, as had been promised, and would be returned to the nursing home on the following day, as my father had requested, so that they could be together when she died.

That night, as my brother and I left the hospital knowing Mom would die within the next several days, this same nurse, whom we had only known for a few days, asked if she could hug us. And in recognition of the pain the three of us had just shared, we stood together in the hallway embracing. The decision no longer felt so impersonal and we no longer felt so very alone. There are no thanks for such a gift. There is only memory and endless gratitude.

47

"There is something both sacred and profane about the moment of death."

SHARING DEATH

There is something both sacred and profane about the moment of death. And those who are present are marked by it. My mother, Evelyn Lieberman, died at her nursing home three weeks ago in my father's arms, surrounded by those who loved her and those who cared for her. The people who brought her to that moment all kept their word and I wish to honor them by acknowledging their help.

When her physician and I spoke just before she died, he explained that his goal was to give his elderly patients the best quality of life and the best quality of death that he could. He promised me that she would feel no discomfort when we removed life-supporting equipment, and he delivered on that promise.

The nursing home staff made me feel ashamed. Ashamed for not recognizing the depth of their caring and the breadth of their skill. When an ambulance returned my mother from the hospital, we knew she was dying. Kathy, the director of nursing, was with the attendants as they wheeled my mother into her room.

Once she was returned, unconscious, to her own bed, my bedridden father asked to be able to hold her and kiss her good-bye. Within three minutes, Kathy had the maintenance staff in the room, moving furniture, lowering safety bars, tying the beds together. The nursing staff immediately rearranged the linens and helped move my parents together. And as the late afternoon sun streamed through the wall of windows in their room, my mother began the final process of dying and my father completed the process of saying good-bye.

My brother and I, also holding Mom, were frightened by some of what we were seeing. Kathy stood right there beside us to explain and reassure us that Mom was not in pain, that the jagged breathing and labored sighs were a normal part of dying. Others on the nursing staff entered and remained during the brief time we held Mom and continued to speak to her. They shared this moment with us as part of the caring community of people who had labored long and hard to give my mother a meaningful life. They comforted family and friends who were present in the room.

And when it was over and Mom was gone, they cried. The nurses and nurse's aides wept openly, embracing my brother and me and each other. Shirley grabbed me and held on for long minutes, repeating, "I'm here for you, I'm here for you," like the chorus of a hymn. Melinda wept in my arms as I said, "I never expected this kind of caring in a nursing home." "Don't say that," she pleaded as she wept, and made me deeply ashamed of my blindness. Andrea stood beside my mother's bed, looked down, and said in a trembling voice, "You're at peace, Mrs. Lieberman," and then she too ran from the room in tears. I ran after her to hug her and tell her it was all right. After giving my father time alone with my mother, with great care and tenderness,

Brenda and others on the staff began to prepare my mother to leave the nursing home.

These were the nurses who had bathed her, helped her to eat, attended to her medications, helped her dress. They had encouraged her, cajoled her, been annoyed with her, answered her questions, teased her good-heartedly, dealt with her demands, and offered her friendship. In a special way, day in and day out, they had been like another family. Some close, some distant, some warm, some cold. But always there. I had counted on them to help Mom, never realizing how much they were also helping me. And perhaps by honoring their work and recognizing what these people did to make this final moment more sacred than profane, I can find a positive meaning in my mother's death.

48

"My father is dying and my brother and I have to let him, have to help him do it."

ROAD MAP: THE ADVANCE DIRECTIVE

I can't believe I am in this dark and cold and lonely place again so soon. My father is dying and my brother and I have to let him, have to help him do it. The bedrock of my philosophy has always been to choose life. But now I find myself asking, "At what cost in suffering?"

After we removed life support from my mother eight weeks ago and allowed her to die as she wished, my father seemed to lose his focus. For the first time, his powerful intellect failed him, his mind began to wander into frightening and ugly places, and he began to see and relate to things that were not really there. He refused to understand and accept that my mother was gone and had terrible hallucinations about where she really was and what she really was doing. He saw snakes in his bed and plastic melting down the walls of his room. It is a special agony to watch a parent's mind begin to die before his body does.

But my father's body wasn't far behind. He developed gangrene, a fungus infection, a bedsore. His weight dropped to 112 pounds. As I watched the doctor place a temporary shunt in his neck to facilitate dialysis, I was horrified at how thin my father had become. His ribs looked as if someone had draped a silk sheet across a skeleton. He developed a blood infection and his temperature shot up to almost 104. When I left him in the hospital two nights ago, he was coughing up blood, incontinent, and mostly incoherent. And I found a sweet and tearing irony in the fact that as I left, telling him I loved him, he whispered, "Me, too. Be careful. Don't worry about me."

Because the primary shunt in his arm had clotted, making dialysis impossible, my father was scheduled to undergo a minor surgical procedure to clear it once his temperature was brought down. If clearing was impossible, the surgeon was going to have to insert another shunt (this had happened twice before), and this was a more invasive operation, though still not major surgery. But it would allow Dad to continue to receive more than ten hours a week of exhausting dialysis.

Both the surgeon and anesthesiologist spoke carefully with my brother and me about Dad's wishes not to be resuscitated if he should go into cardiac arrest during the surgical procedure, and they laid out the options and prognosis of recurring shunt complications. When we were all clear about what Dad had said he wanted, we kissed him and went out to the waiting room. And as we were sitting down, my brother and I looked at each other and said, "Why are we doing this?"

Clearly we were only saving Dad for further agony. And he had told both of us he did not want to continue living when the burdens to him became greater than the benefits, when he could no longer think with consistent clarity. Were we at that place? Was it time for us to implement my father's advance directive and tell the surgeon not to operate, to allow Dad to stop dialysis and to die? My brother and I spent a long moment searching each other's faces for consensus and found it.

Racing back to the surgical desk, we asked to speak with the doctor. He emerged, already dressed in his operating scrubs. We told him of our decision to cancel the surgery and he agreed immediately, telling us this is what he had wanted to recommend but could not. He could only propose it as an option and wait for our instructions. Then he telephoned the nephrologist who has been dialyzing my father weekly for the past two years. This doctor also validated our decision to cancel surgery, citing my father's physical suffering and the continuing strain of dialysis on an eighty-two-year-old man who was clearly dying. The anesthesiologist joined us and concurred, saying that my father's discussions with us about his wishes and the advance directive he had signed were a great gift to his children. They promised to keep my father pain free for the few remaining days of his life, and then the decision became reality as they wheeled my father back to his room.

This morning I awoke at 5 A.M. thinking, "My father is dying." A part of me is torn with grief. But I would be less than honest if I didn't admit that another part of me is relieved and grateful that he gave me a mechanism to end his awful suffering. Over the next few days, my brother and I will spend the hours with Dad: holding him, talking with him when he is awake and aware, and talking with each other when he is not. This is a healing time for us as well.

For the past two years, my mother, my father, my brother, and I have traveled an extraordinary road together as we journeyed toward the final moments of Milton and Evelyn Lieberman. Extraordinary not because it is an uncommon path. To the contrary, it is a universal path. A parent's death is a universally intimate, personal, and private moment. It comes to most of us.

It has been an extraordinary journey because we have had no map, yet we were tightly confined and bound by our biological links. Extraordinary because we have had to maneuver within the limits of the relationships we had forged over the past fifty-four years. Extraordinary because we, at times, have loved and hated each other. And because none of us knew exactly how to get where we were going.

Within the next few days my father will die, and my parents, my brother, and I will have arrived at our destination. It has been a rough trip. We have open wounds. We have scars. And we have memories, some very good. At times, traveling with my parents into their old age has felt like a forced march. Often I have not wanted to go. But it gives me great satisfaction that we have dealt with the roadblocks, followed the detours, found the route, and made this trip together. When my father dies, my parents will have arrived and I will have visited the place where we all are going. Although the route differs for each family, in the struggle to find the way I think we feel the same pain.

49

"What if I go home tonight and he dies?"

WHEN THE QUESTION IS AN ANSWER

It is over. I spent the final day of my father's life alongside his bed, watching him breathe easily, counting his heart beats by watching the vein in his neck swell and recede. He was not aware of my presence, but I was extraordinarily aware of his.

I remember how peaceful he looked, the antiseptic hospital odors that surrounded him. And I remember acutely the passage of time. But most of all, I remember the question. After a dawn-to-dusk day at the hospital, I stood at the foot of his bed and tried to decide whether or not to go home that evening. I wrestled with an old, old enemy—what if. What if I go home tonight and he dies? How will I feel? What if I stay here all night and his coma persists? What will I do? How long can I be here without going home?

No one knew how long he would continue to live. I had been at his bedside for several days. The waiting was the total focus of my life. Everything else receded into a hazy blur. We sat quietly together. But I needed to sleep and eat and touch my family. So I asked the question, confronted the what-ifs, and decided to spend the night at home.

The call came at 1:15 A.M. He had died peacefully and alone. My husband and I met my brother at the hospital at 2 A.M. and we marked the end of our vigil by comforting each other and talking quietly about the end of his life and the continuance of ours.

In the midst of the myriad emotions that accompany the loss of a parent, I found myself searching for one that I did not find . . . regret about my decision to go home that evening. I expected it. I looked for it. And I came to an extraordinary understanding. The question I had asked myself as I stood at the foot of his bed and counted his breaths was more important than the answer. I had confronted the issue, thought about it, and made a decision. That was what counted.

Was it the right decision? I'm still not sure. There's a part of me that would have liked to have been with him. And there's a part of me that did not want to be there in his final moments. We had loved each other long and hard, and he wasn't always an easy man to understand. We had been together through many illnesses. I had nothing left to prove to him. But did I need to prove something to myself? I don't think so. What continues to haunt me is the crucial importance of the question I had asked myself. I am so grateful that I thought about it, explored it, considered the possible outcomes.

This week I will celebrate my fifty-fifth birthday, the first one since the loss of my parents. And in a strange irony, the final lesson I learned from my father, a man who would have made a wonderful teacher but had spent his life as a businessman instead, is that the question sometimes means more than the answer.

PART IV

Dawn

Grief

With the dawning of grief comes the promise of survival. As darkness recedes we can once again see pathways. Grief is a well-worn trail, and the blaze marks left by others are helpful because I feel so lost. Much of what I feel is not sad and I do not recognize the signs of my mourning. I must learn what grieving is and how to do it.

There are surprises. There is new learning about old feelings. Pain often accompanies the unexpected pleasures of remembering. There is evaluation and questioning and judgment: "Did I say what I wanted? Did I do the right things? Did I make the right decisions?" Regret and sadness live alongside guilt and uncertainty as the healing process begins. And spasms of sorrow punctuate my life for a long time. The rituals of closing a life are enormously difficult. My parents' possessions and the paperwork vie with the pain for time and space in my life. Relief feels wrong.

Love is no longer a dialogue between my parents and me. We cannot spar for each other's attention and affection. It is a conversation I now carry on with myself, an internal processing. Did I? Did they? Did we? The good-bye lasts a long time and it is lonely work.

50

"How can I miss what I hated doing?"

CAREGIVER WITHDRAWAL

So much is gone. My father died on October 10, and now, ten days later, it feels as if I am groping in a darkened room filled with booby traps. Death didn't frighten me. I had faced it eight weeks earlier as I watched my mother die. What I was unprepared for was missing what I had hated doing.

Missing may not be the right word. Perhaps "letting go" is more descriptive. Visiting my parents at the nursing home was very difficult. As their bodies broke down and became more painful to live in, I saw my parents struggle to keep their minds intact. It sometimes felt as if I were watching a superhero from my childhood lose in mortal combat. Didn't Captain Marvel and Wonder Woman always win in the end? They never bled. They never complained. They never died.

But Mom and Dad did all of these things. Now, each day, I drive home from work and pass the street that I turned down to go to the nursing home. And mixed with my relief at not having to go there is a tug to make that right turn. My parents are no longer at the end of that road. How can I miss what I hated doing?

My parents had very specific expectations and very rigid needs. Shopping for the exact kind of hand lotion (Jergens with vitamin E *and* aloe), and the exact kind of diaper (Depends *without* elastic legs), and the exact flavor of toothpaste (Crest mint flavored), and the exact kind of toilet water (Jontue) was an inconvenient, frustrating chore as my brother and I went from drugstore to supermarket to department store trying to accommodate their precise requests. If it wasn't the right one, in the right size, we had to take it back. I pass the shopping center near the nursing home now and I remember the nighttime stops after work and the searches for the things I knew they were waiting for. How can I miss what I hated doing?

After my father's funeral, my brother asked me if I thought I would have "caregiver withdrawal," and I almost laughed at the idea. I'm not laughing now. I'm struggling to define the strange feelings that accompany my memories of all the things that were so hard to do. And I am trying to learn how to let go of some memories and accept the relief that I feel without guilt.

An acquaintance wisely suggested that my journey is not yet over, and shared the fact that she continued to get to know and understand her mother long after her mother had died. I think she is right and I am grateful for her advice. I still have much to learn about both my parents and myself. And the first thing I have learned without them is that the journey continues.

51

"I have to learn what grief is and how to do it."

SURVIVING DEATH

Grief has come. This is my first real time at it and I'm a novice. It's like trying to play a game without knowing the rules. I'm on the playing field and things are happening all around me. I don't understand what's going on, what comes next, and what I need to do to move the action along. I have to learn what grief is and how to do it.

Since Mom and Dad became ill over a period of years, I had time to brace myself for their deaths. Time to say, "I love you." Time to do what I needed to do, what I wanted to do. I had time to come to closure, to deal with many issues long repressed. I had time, and I didn't always accomplish all these things. But I tried, and trying felt good.

And then they died. I wept, followed the rituals of my faith, gratefully accepted the comfort of friends, family, and caring strangers. And at the end of the prescribed period of grieving, I went back to my life, back to being a wife and mother. Back to my job. I returned to a long-neglected focus on my own agenda. And I felt sad, but not anguished.

"How come?" I wondered. Where was all the horrible grief I had braced myself for? I worried that I might be repressing it and had a four-hour dinner with a friend who is a therapist to find out if I was OK. She said I was and we talked about how my grieving had begun years before my parents died. And so life seemed to return to some kind of normalcy. I went to work. I cooked dinner. I enjoyed life. I didn't understand what was happening to me until last week.

I met a woman at a professional meeting who confided that she had recently lost an adult child. I shared my own recent losses with her. "How are you doing with your grief?" she asked. "OK, I think," I responded. "What's your life like now?" she probed. "Well, I'm back at work. Tired, but slowly getting the work out. But I really find it difficult to focus." Her eyes lit up. "Grief will do that to you," she said, and launched into what she had learned from the bereavement groups she had participated in. "You may get more physically ill than is usual for you at this time of year, may feel more aches and pains, may be having trouble sleeping."

"Yes," I thought, "I have some of these problems." But I had never linked them to grief. When I got home from the meeting, I called my brother and we began to just talk with each other about our lives, about our memories, about the past two months. Separated for the past twenty-five years by the five hundred miles between Maryland and Massachusetts, we had had limited opportunity to bond as adults.

"You know," he said after a long pause, "I've been feeling lazy when I can't focus on work, feeling like I *should* be able to get this behind me and move on, meet my deadlines, get back into the harness." "Yesssss!!" I was so grateful that he understood exactly how I was feeling. I had been privately horrified at my own difficulties picking up the pieces: getting my job done, getting my laundry done, getting dinner done. "C'mon, Judy," I had told myself. "This should be easier now that the pressure is off for caring for Mom and Dad." My brother and I have been seriously unforgiving of ourselves out of ignorance.

"So this is what grief feels like," I found myself saying to him. And we agreed that we hadn't recognized it, didn't even know that these things were part of the process. He's just gotten over the worst case of bronchitis he's ever had. I've been dealing with aches and pains in new places. But because these things didn't feel *sad,* we had not associated them with grief. I thought grief would be crying, memories, a sense of loss. I wasn't expecting physical pain, inability to concentrate, difficulty sleeping.

And so I have decided to try to slow down a bit and get to know my grief. To cut myself some slack when focus fails me. To recognize a new meaning in some old feelings. To allow myself extra time to do things that are hard. To be forgiving. And most of all to stop blaming myself, to stop calling grief incompetence.

52

"It feels very strange to celebrate without her."

THE GIFT OF REMEMBERING

The date snuck up on me, and today I realized that my mother can never be eighty-two. Yesterday, November 3, would have been her eighty-second birthday and she died eighty-eight days ago. That shocks me because I thought her death happened yesterday. I think it will always feel like yesterday. I was with her when she died and the image remains. There is no delete button that can wipe it from my memory.

I spent November 3 thinking about my mother . . . when I was at work . . . when I ate lunch . . . when I drove home . . . after dinner . . . before bed. It is ironic because before she died I could never remember the exact date of her birthday. It was always fodder for family discussion. Mom said that she was born on November 3, but that her birth certificate read November 5. So the date was always hazy to me. I just knew it was the first week in November and purchased gifts accordingly.

I used to think there was some deeply hidden mother-daughter angst that prevented me from remembering which day was her birthday. But yesterday, in the replay of memory, I realized that part of why I couldn't remember Mom's birthday was because she was not a celebrationist. She wouldn't encourage or allow a big fuss to be made . . . or any fuss for that matter. For me, sometimes, that made the day more painful than pleasurable. I will celebrate anything good in a heartbeat. Mom was different.

So I agonized over the gifts I gave her. Often she asked me to take back what I had selected. My mother made celebrating hard. But yesterday it was easy to celebrate her life in my mind. There was no one I needed to satisfy but myself. And so I have been thinking of my mother and trying to better understand and appreciate who she was.

It feels very strange to celebrate without her. To mark the

day without sharing it with her. Over the past two months, I have learned some surprising things about my mother from her cousins in New York. I hadn't seen or spoken with them in forty years, but they called when they learned Mom had died, and it was wonderful to share their memories. I discovered that the organized, rigid, and dependable woman I knew as my mother had been a funny, mischievous twelve-year-old who had stripped naked in front of her cousin Jean's bedroom window, airily telling a horrified Jean that "It doesn't matter to me . . . the neighbors will think it's you."

Jean talked about how my mother was pressured by her father to leave high school before graduation because "girls need to work to support themselves, not get an education" . . . that was more important for boys. No wonder my mother was sensitive about her past. A very bright woman, an avid reader and crossword puzzler (she did them in ink!), she had never graduated from high school. I had never heard the whole story.

"Your mother never got an allowance when she was a child," Jean explained, "and she went to work very young to make money to buy herself clothing, because her father didn't want to pay." No wonder Mom fixated on clothes when she was middle-aged. From the time I was born until I married, Mom always saw to it that I had lovely things to wear . . . a beautiful new dress for a high school dance, a smart new suit for a teenage job search, a new wardrobe every spring. And once I was on my own, she focused a great deal of energy on dressing herself.

It used to irritate me as a young mother struggling with three small children when she would say, "You should buy yourself some clothes." I always took that as a criticism of what I was wearing. I never had the frame of reference Jean provided. I never understood, because my mother never shared her stories, never spoke about her childhood or youth.

So on this day, I have chosen to celebrate my mother, not only as I knew her, but also as she recently has been explained to me. And now I recognize even more how important it is to share stories of my life, my childhood, my memories, with my children. It gives them a context in which to place me. It gives them a beginning to add to the middle they already know about me as we travel together toward my end. And today I finally found the perfect gift to give my mother on her birthday each November 3. It can't be returned. It's never the wrong size or color. It will always fit. It is the gift of understanding, appreciating, and remembering.

53

"Our parents live rent-free in our heads forever."

SEEING DAD AGAIN

Michael said it would happen, and it did. I was riding the Metro into downtown D.C. A few stops after I got on, the train arrived at a station, and a crowd of people burst through the door letting in the cold winter air. Then I saw the man, the man Michael (a friend from work) had told me about. An older man, with a ring of longish white hair around a shiny tan dome and a bushy white mustache. He was about five feet six, a little stooped, wearing a nondescript khaki raincoat. He sat across the aisle from me, several seats ahead, and I felt myself staring intently at the back of his head. It was my father. He looked so much like my father.

But of course, my father died two months ago. And Michael had told me this would happen. Michael lost his father in the summer, and we had occasionally shared our mutual suffering at the office when the phones were still and the workload allowed an intimate moment.

"One day," Michael prophesied, leaning across his desk with an intense look in his very dark brown eyes, "you'll be just living your life and you'll see someone walking down the street who looks familiar . . . the same bald spot, the same height, the same kind of walk. And for a moment, you'll think it's your father."

I sat on the train, lulled by the rhythmic rocking as it sped from the sunlight of Silver Spring into the work-world darkness of underground Washington. I was so focused on the man across the aisle, I was afraid he could feel my staring. I kept leaning forward in my seat, trying to get a better look at his face. The mustache was so familiar. Same forehead. Same eyebrows. I closed my eyes and pictured my father. It's amazing to me how much I remember about his physical presence. I guess part of that is because before he died I spent a week watching him in the hospital. I sat for hours at his bedside studying his face, watching the vein in his neck thicken with each heartbeat, listening to him breathe, memorizing his features. I knew I was saying good-bye to him.

And now I realize that as we live our lives alongside our parents, periodically, without our even activating it, something presses the record button, and we have a freeze frame. Maybe it's a moment of high emotion: maybe it's anger, maybe it's love. I remember the day my father learned he would have to begin dialysis. It's not fear or anxiety that I remember. Or even his stoic resignation. It's simply the way he looked. It's the quality of the light in the hospital hallway as the sunshine drenched his gown and turned his ring of hair into a silver band. Did I choose that moment to remember? Or did the vision of my father sitting in the sunshine move me so profoundly that I kept it in my mind without deciding to?

I have a saying taped over my desk. A good friend shared it with me several years ago in a moment of mutual hilarity as we fiftysomethings compared our struggles to come to terms with being the middle-aged children of aging parents. "Our parents live rent-free in our heads forever!" she declared with exasperation as she talked about still feeling the power of her mother's unspoken demands, the guilt, the frustration, the ambivalent love.

We laughed together that day, coconspirators still negotiating the separation that is vital for children to complete in preparation for the final separation that comes with death. But as I sat on the train and watched the man who could have been my father, I silently thanked Michael for preparing me, for helping me understand that this is normal, that it happens to other people too. And I also realized that my friend was right. Our parents do live rent free in our heads forever, and also in our hearts.

54

"Sometimes it was hard to be siblings.
Sometimes it was hard to be friends."

PHONE FEAR

My brother answered the phone, and the fear was gone from his voice. It had been around for a long time and finally it had disappeared. I always felt bad when I heard it. I was always sorry to cause it. But I couldn't do anything about it. The fear had become a part of our lives.

While my parents were alive, every time I called my brother, as soon as he heard my voice he braced himself. It got worse as Mom and Dad got older. As the one who spoke with all the doctors, I had the frustrating task of sharing the news, of keeping everyone (including my parents) informed. And I think that for my brother and for me, this bred a kill-the-messenger mentality.

He would answer the phone, his voice reflecting the happiness in his life, and I would wipe the smile out of his world. There had to be surgery, Mom had to go to the eye doctor, Dad needed a blood test, there was a financial problem. Even though we tried to share the responsibilities, squeezing our parents' health needs into our already overcommitted lives was hard for both of us. Sometimes it was hard to be siblings. Sometimes it was hard to be friends. And after planning and sharing two funerals, my brother and I were suddenly left without the late-night emergency calls, without the doctors to talk with, without the need to make sure Mom and Dad had enough of what it took to keep them happy and alive.

That's when the phone fear disappeared. Now I could call him only when I wanted to, not when I needed to. Now we could focus on sharing more of each other's lives and not just crowd that in as an afterthought. I could begin a conversation with "How're the kids?" not just tag that onto the end of an urgent medical message.

I don't know how many other families experience this, but I have spoken with several colleagues who are not the "child of record," as I was. They have shared their feelings about receiving the calls from their brothers and sisters and the difficulty of negotiating this delicate relationship. And I have shared with them what it is like to have to make those calls.

In the time since my parents died, as I continue to work through the feelings that are the fallout of such intense experiences and responsibilities, I find certain things are a relief. Like not having to fit hospital visits and doctors' appointments into a forty-hour workweek. Like not having to negotiate the insurance and Medicaid maze. Like not having to call my brother with unwelcome news. Although the pain of loss is still fresh, it is eased by the reduction in responsibilities. Though I miss my parents, I have a new connection and different relationship with my brother.

In one of the countless hours my husband has spent helping me negotiate this passage through parent care, he shared with me something he had learned from his own experience. "Sometimes," he said, "we don't realize how much some things hurt until we stop doing them." He's right. I remember that every time I pick up the phone to call my brother.

55

"Why do I miss their warnings?"

RECOGNIZING LOSSES

It happened again. I didn't know it was coming. Maybe I'll never know when it's coming. It's blizzarding outside, huge amounts of snow. My neighborhood looks cocooned, wrapped in a soft white mantle that insulates us from each other while at the same time making us feel warm, safe, and connected. People are calling to check on those they care about. And I can't call my parents.

This is the first real snow since they died about three months ago. I have been thinking of them today, and what they might have been doing if they were here. They would have been calling me, worried about me and my family, warning us to get food and stay out of the snow. And I would have hated their apprehension, their fear, their paranoia about the weather and my safety. Then why am I sitting here crying? Why do I miss their warnings?

I guess that's why I called my mother's best friend just a few minutes ago . . . to check on her and her husband as I would have done with my parents. And right in the middle of a perfectly ordinary phone call, I started to cry. My mother's friend Helen understood perfectly. "I miss the phone calls too." She and my mother had spoken to each other daily for fifty-four years. I know that because they met in the delivery room on the day that her daughter (my best friend) and I were born.

Mom was always warning me. It was as if life frightened her and she wanted to protect me from what she was afraid of. And I hated always having to reassure her that, yes, I had enough food in the house. And no, I wasn't stupid and wouldn't try to drive in the heavy snow. My mother's love often came in doses of fear and alarm. Descartes said "I think, therefore I am." With my mother, it was, "I love, therefore I worry." And often I resented the burden of having to constantly reassure her . . . that I was prepared . . . that I wasn't foolish . . . that I had common sense.

Maybe it's those very feelings we had most strongly—feelings of love, anger, resentment—that come back to grab us once someone close to us has died. I guess what is surprising to me when they appear is the feeling of loss . . . of missing even the "bad" feelings. When she was alive I can remember so clearly thinking, if I just didn't have to deal with Mom's angst on top of my own, what a relief it would be. And here I sit, missing her angst.

The flip side of this is that there is comfort in realizing

that I really did love my mother. Sometimes, in all honesty, I wondered. I miss her now in strange ways. I guess when you live your life alongside someone for such a long time and become so familiar with who and what they are, the strong feelings that accompany just living in their company become jumbled together . . . I loved her caring, I hated her warnings, I rejected her fears for me. I really just lived those feelings while she was here and never tried to sort them out. I felt them but did not have (or take) the time to think about them very much.

Now I have the time. And I find that when they strike I will take them apart, look at them, think about them, feel them, and then find (I hope) a place in the archive of my mind in which to store them safely until the next time I want to retrieve them. And so I sit at my window, typing these words as the snow swirls around the trees, and think, yes, Mom, I have food in the house. No, Mom, I won't go out driving. And thanks, Mom. I miss you.

56

"We borrow in advance on our energy,
but we pay back the loan with great interest."

LIFE'S OVERDRAFT PRIVILEGES

Ivey looked so tired as she sat in front of her computer. A beautiful young woman with long, curling, chocolate-colored hair and warm, sympathetic eyes, she was usually the carbonation that bubbled through our office giving the day just the right amount of effervescence. But not today. Lugging my briefcase into her cubicle, I stopped to say good night. "You look really exhausted," I said. "Are you feeling OK?" She told me she was. "It's just that I'm so tired lately," she added. And then things clicked into place.

"You're overdrawn at the bank," I said, and Ivey looked up questioningly. I explained my theory about the interest we pay on the energy loans we take out. About a month ago, Ivey's mother had been critically ill and I had watched Ivey race back and forth between the hospital and the office. Her phone calls to doctors and to reassure family members had struck a very familiar chord as I remembered my own journey through the illnesses of my parents.

Being almost five months on the other side of this experience, I recognized the symptoms of overdrawing from one's energy reserves. As I look back now on my parents' final illnesses, I am amazed at how I kept all the plates in my life spinning. I remember running from my daughter plate to my parent plate to my wife plate to my office plate to my sister plate to my friend plate. I must have looked like a madwoman sometimes, wildly racing around from one to another, touching each just enough to keep it balanced and spinning. You pay for this work.

My husband and I talked about Ivey that evening. I was worried about her. "It's a good thing life gives us overdraft privileges," I began as we ended dinner over steaming cups of tea. Everyone has crises in their lives. And we usually rise to the occasion, whether it's the loss of a person, a job, or a dream. People seem to gather their resources and bring them to the battle. What I didn't realize until after both of my parents died is that we borrow in advance on our energy, but we pay back the loan with great interest. I'm still making payments.

Yesterday Ivey spent the day at the hospital with her mother, who was having some postoperative tests. I called her in the evening. Test results had been good and she sounded relieved. Some of the sparkle had returned to her voice. "Be kind to yourself," I said, echoing the wisdom of an experienced and generous friend who had counseled me as I went through my own borrowing. "Take the time to rest. Allow yourself to slow down. Cut yourself some slack at home and at work. It can take months to feel rested again." And I remembered clearly when that had been said to me. I knew how much energy I had expended and what I needed. But somehow it helped to hear it from someone else. It was almost as if I needed permission to slow down and take care of myself. I did slow down and I hope Ivey will.

We make these loans because of who we are and whom we love. We make them on behalf of our husbands, our wives, our children, our parents, and our friends. Sometimes the debt grows to be enormous. And because we don't write out monthly checks as reminders, we often forget that we are paying on that loan. There is no paper trail to remind us of the installments. And often there is no recognizable moment of closure when we know we are no longer in debt.

But there are signs. Just this week I felt restored enough to begin to respond to the wonderful outpouring of support I received when my parents died. I began to answer the letters I treasure. It feels good to be reducing my energy debt with Saturday afternoon matinees, Sunday morning sleep-ins, a good book, a new piece of needlework, a weekend with the kids. I'm resting—not rested, but on the way to getting there.

57

"Some day spring will come and I won't be here, but you will."

THE NATURAL ORDER OF THINGS

As winter sputters to a halt and spring asserts itself, I am apprehensive about the swelling buds on the trees and the coming of flowers. For with them comes a memory of the day my father predicted my first spring without him. It was a soft and balmy day in April, and I had the unexpected time for an afternoon visit with my parents. I had forgotten that it was a day that Dad had dialysis, and as I walked up to the front door, I found him sitting in the sunshine amid a profusion of flowers as he waited in his wheelchair for the special van to pick him up.

There was no place to sit down, so I stood in front of him and we talked—about the weather, about the season, about our lives. He was relaxed and smiling, but he looked very old. "You know," he said slowly, looking around and savoring the color and the fragrance of the day, "some day spring will come and I won't be here, but you will." I felt my eyes fill with tears as he spoke.

"And that's as it should be," he continued, giving me a gift he knew I would need. At that moment, I made a conscious decision to let my father see my sorrow. "I want him to know that I'll miss him," I thought, as we shared the sunshine. My tears spoke the words that I could not. I moved beside his wheelchair and rested my hand on his bruised, knotty arm because the physical contact seemed to give us another pathway of communication. And so we waited together, speaking to each other silently.

He was right. Now the buds are coming again, and he is not here. Just as he predicted. "And that's as it should be," I say to comfort myself, as his voice echoes through the corridors of my memory.

I think about the natural order of things: we are born, we grow, we may marry, we may have children, we age, we die. And in between those things, and amid those milestones, we live our daily lives. My father and I were part of the same continuum as the trees and blossoms that surrounded us, I in the early fall of my life and he in his winter. He died six months later, when nature was orchestrating an amazing autumn crescendo of color before its own rest.

But I remember that spring day with a special clarity. It was one of those rare moments when my father and I understood each other perfectly and said a good-bye to each other with special fondness. And that too was as it should be.

58

"Do you miss your dad more than your mom?"

MISSING PARENTS DIFFERENTLY

Last week I was really sick and I missed my mother. I missed her always being there. And by "there" I don't mean a physical presence. She was not the kind of woman who fussed over her children. There were many things she didn't do that I desperately wish she had. But as a child, when I was sick she was always beside me, comforting, coddling, and caring. And at the age of fifty-four as I lay in bed tossing and turning with a fever, achy and feeling awful, I missed her ministrations and her worry.

It shocked me when the thought popped into my head: this is the first time I have been really sick since my mother died and somehow it feels lonely. I played with it for the entire week as I recovered from a vile virus. And on the first day I felt well enough to pad into the kitchen and look for some hot soup, I called my mother's best friend, Helen, and we talked . . . about many inconsequential things.

Finally I worked up the courage to tell her how much I was missing Mom. It sounds funny to talk in terms of courage, but I thought about telling her for a long time during our conversation before I did it. I wasn't sure I had a tight enough grip on my emotions. And sure enough, as I said it I could hear the quiver in my own voice. But it was comforting to hear the compassion in hers, and I was able to talk my way through the pain.

Later that day, I was on the phone with a casual friend and she asked me a personal question, which she assured me I didn't have to answer. "Do you miss your dad more than your mom? It seems that you were closer to him than to her." Given my earlier conversation with Helen, the question was interesting and I guess I was primed.

"I miss them in different ways because I knew them in different ways," I began, as I explored the feelings that the question unleashed. My father and I had spent the fifty-four years we had together talking about our philosophies, sharing ideas, visiting art galleries together, being dreamers. My mother was grounded in practicalities. She taught me to iron, to cook, to crochet. We talked about things rather than ideas. He loved books about information, she loved books about stories. I love both kinds of books.

Did I love one parent more than the other? Maybe. Was I closer to one than the other? Perhaps. Do I miss them equally? I miss them differently. Being sick made me realize that.

Helen understood. When our conversation had wound down, she touched me deeply and filled a very empty hole when she cautioned, "And tomorrow, if you still have temperature, stay home from work! That's what your mother would have told you, isn't it?" my mother's best friend said.

59

"I remember her apple pie, her immaculate house, her ability to organize, and the enormous novels she loved to read."

THE MEMORIES WE SELECT

The colors caught my attention and the cards caught me by surprise. I was making a late-night run to the grocery store and was headed for the express checkout when I saw them. Mother's Day cards. This would be the first time in all my memory that I didn't have to think about buying or making one. A habit of some fifty years is hard to break.

When my mother died last August, I had heard about how hard the first year of grieving is. I braced myself for birthdays, for holidays, for the pain of memory. And, to be truthful, some times hurt more than others. The first snowstorm without my mother around to warn me about being careful hurt more than her first birthday. And the first time I was sick without her to worry about me hurt more than missing her on Thanksgiving. I find that I miss her painfully for very unexpected reasons. Not at all what I had prepared myself for.

I think much of a person's grieving must be related to the kind of relationship he or she had with the lost loved one. And so each grief must be individual. The pain is not different: we miss the person, wish they were still with us, feel the emptiness. But maybe what triggers that grieving feeling differs with each person. I don't know. I'm just guessing.

My encounter in the grocery store opened the door to several weeks of quiet thinking about past Mother's Days. I remember when I was seven spending my twenty-five-cent allowance on garish glass and paste jewelry in the dime store and presenting her with what I thought was an elegant piece of jewelry. My mother accepted it with appreciation and pride. When I was older, I remember buying her clothes she never wore and things she never used. And most of all, I remember her repaired dental plate—my last Mother's Day gift to her.

When I saw the pink and white cards at the checkout counter and realized that Mother's Day was approaching, I had very mixed feelings. It was hard to be honest with myself because some of the feelings seemed contradictory. Sadness at not having her here to celebrate. Relief at not having to shop for a gift for someone who often was very hard to please. Nostalgia for past Mother's Days. Anticipation of my own first Mother's Day as the sole focus of family attention. "Were these feelings OK?" I found myself wondering. "Do other people in my situation have them? How could I celebrate my mother's life and keep her in mine?"

While I was out walking today in the beautiful spring weather, I found an answer. I will celebrate her by remembering as many really good things as I can recall. Her apple pie. Her chopped liver. The way she made my favorite dish, roast leg of lamb. Her immaculate house. The smell of fresh linens on my childhood bed. The fact that even while I was in college and living at home, she did my laundry, vacuumed my room, and made my bed. Her ability to organize. The dazzling afghans she crocheted for everyone in my family.

The enormous novels she loved to read. Her bright eyes and young voice, even at the age of eighty. The funny way she got my brother and me to eat spinach when we were little by mixing it with mashed potatoes and topping it with a blob of ketchup. The crispy, crunchy sandwiches she made on an always toasted kaiser roll. Shopping with her for prom and party dresses. Drying the dishes with her when she washed, talking about my teenage life.

So this is the gift I have decided to share with my mother each Mother's Day from now on—the gift of remembering all the good things that happened in the fifty-four years we spent together. It's not expensive. It will always fit. It cannot be taken back. It's never in the wrong color. I promise myself always to make the time to do it. And I am guessing, from the way I feel today, that in doing this, I will strengthen the good memories of my mother and begin to forget the conflicts we had and the difficult circumstances of her death. Of all the things you gave me, Mom, these are among the simplest and the best. Happy Mother's Day.

60

"After the initial agony, the pain subsided."

HOW WE HEAL

From the time I was little, I've watched my body heal. Especially my knees. Maybe I was a klutzy kid, but I have fifty-year-old scars on my knees that are the history of my childhood and a testimony to Mercurochrome and the healing process.

However, my most famous scar is on my ankle, earned when I was forty-seven and precipitated by my Thanksgiving turkey. Taking the twenty-six-pound steaming bird out of the oven, brimful of toasted stuffing and gloriously golden, I spilled hot fat into my shoe. A crescent-shaped blister about three inches wide swelled up as the fat lay smoldering and soaking into my sneaker. After the initial agony, the pain subsided. I cleaned up my shoe and ankle and was able to enjoy Thanksgiving. But later that night as I undressed for bed, I saw the enormous blister on my ankle and was horrified. It didn't hurt anymore; it just looked red, raw, and angry.

I saw my doctor the following day and he immediately sent me to a plastic surgeon. He examined the blister and explained that I would have to see him every week for a period of time so that he could determine how it was healing and whether or not I would need a skin graft. Skin graft? I had had no idea that the burn had been so severe.

And so I began a long series of weekly treks to the surgeon, who unwrapped the bandage on my ankle carefully, took a good look, and pronounced it healing. But it was a different kind of healing than I was used to seeing. No scab. A bad burn heals from around the edges, slowly . . . very slowly. So slowly that you can hardly see the difference from week to week. Imperceptibly, the edges of healthy skin regenerate, and like a puddle drying up, the raw middle grows less and less so until the edges of the burn meet and close. Until that final closure, there is always a raw spot and always the danger of infection.

Perhaps the mind and spirit mimic the body. This week I thought about how grief is a healing process as well, an almost invisible regeneration of spirit around a raw and painful wound. In the spirit of my religious tradition, I have begun to plan the unveiling of the memorial plaques to mark the graves of both of my parents. My healing process has been so slow as to be almost imperceptible during the past ten months. But I realize as I face this final task that it will represent closure. The edges of the wound will have come together.

Scar tissue is strong tissue, I have been told. Scars mark traumatic events, record them on our bodies, as the death of a parent scars our souls, leaving an indelible mark. But life is programmed to heal, and I have made the decision to think of that mark as symbolic of regeneration and as a mandate to live life as fully and well as I can.

61

"I would sit at her kitchen table waiting for cream cheese cookies and juice glasses."

FINDING THE UNIVERSAL IN THE PARTICULAR

Today I take my place in the endless line of people who ritually memorialize their dead parents. Metaphorically looking behind myself, I can sense the queue stretching endlessly beyond the horizon, wrapping itself around the world multiple times in a mantle of honored memory. Today, in the spirit of my religious tradition, I light a candle that will burn for twenty-four hours in memory of my mother.

It's hard to believe that a year has passed since her death. And strange as it seems, as I approached this day, I spent a great deal of time thinking about my grandmother's juice glasses. My mother's mother and father lived in New York. And every Easter vacation, when school let out, we packed our new spring outfits and took the train to visit. It was an exciting time for me: riding the train, eating breakfast in the dining car, anticipating seeing my cousins, playing stoop-ball on Sixty-fifth Street in Brooklyn.

My grandfather was always hanging out of the second-floor sun-parlor window of the two-story row house that was a stamp of all the others on their block. He was watching out for us, elbows on the sill, eyes following every car that passed. And as we clambered up the tall staircase that led to their apartment, I knew certain things would always be there: the framed silhouette of Abraham Lincoln on the wall by the phone, the dining room chairs with the hearts carved out in the back, and the juice glasses.

My grandparents were very solid and simple people. A carpenter, my grandfather had retired even before I was born. My grandmother, a homemaker, was a woman who had aged into a beautiful, white-haired, blue-eyed lady of tiny stature. She'd sit in her kitchen peeling oranges in long strips of rind that she would give me to wear as a bracelet. And my brother and I would sit at the table waiting for her special cream cheese cookies and glasses of cold milk in the juice glasses.

She had a huge set of these glasses. They were very plain with a design of arches pressed into the glass. And as the cold milk slid down with the melt-in-your-mouth cookies, I had no idea that I was drinking from the cup of my grandmother's memories. The glasses she so frugally saved were the containers that had held the memorial candles she lit for her parents each year . . . as my mother did for her . . . as I am doing today for my mother . . . as my children will one day do for me.

And so yesterday, on the phone, my brother and I joked about the glasses, remembering all the minutiae of those vacation visits. We sought comfort in each other's memories as we faced the task of taking our place in that long line of ritual.

I have long felt that it is the writer's job and joy to seek the universal in the particular, to look at the everyday things in this world and sense their greater meaning, and to connect with other people through this understanding. So it is with both apprehension and approval that I light the "yahrzeit" (year time) candle for my mother. Because if I am doing this, I must be getting older. If I am doing this, I must have cause to honor my mother. If I am doing this, I have lived through a year of my life without my mother in it. If I am doing this, I am remembering. And through the juice glasses, I am remembering and honoring people I never knew. People whose choice to have children gave rise to me.

When the candle is burned down, I won't save the glass. My cupboards are full. But I will savor the memories. And isn't that the reason for the traditions we select to follow?

62

"Closure is both an ending and a beginning."

SAYING THANKS AND GOOD-BYE

One final rite of passage, called for by my faith, drew me once again to the cemetery. I had not been there for almost a year and I wondered, as I drove into Virginia, what it would feel like to stand once again before the graves of my parents and speak my heart. Twelve months had passed, and it was both timely and traditional to place and unveil the bronze marker I had chosen for their graves. In my pocket I carried letters I had written to each of them that reviewed and revered the relationships we had fashioned with each other. Family and friends would join us and had been invited to contribute their memories to the occasion as well.

The letter to my father was one I had written on his eightieth birthday, two years before his death, and two days before he entered the nursing home. The letter to my mother I wrote only two days ago, almost exactly a year and one month since she died. I have chosen to share them here because in writing them, and in speaking them aloud before family and friends, I found a comforting sense that I was approaching closure on a very important and intimate part of my life. I think I would have felt the same even if no one else had been present, because I have begun to understand that closure doesn't just happen. It has to be worked toward. Closure is both an ending and a beginning.

Dear Dad,

I spent the day with you today, watching you dismantle a lifetime accumulation of duties and desires, deconstruct your home, triage long-held treasures. It must have been difficult for you, but for me it reinforced who you really are. When you get into a man's underwear drawer and go through all his files, you are seeing the core person.

It gave me pause to think about what is obviously important to you: your books, your photographs, your slides, your collection of clippings and files of facts. You are not, and never were, a social animal. But you are an intellectual investigator.

You are an unobtrusive observer at the world's table, rarely a physical presence but always there: reading about art, clipping newspapers, taping programs. The exigencies of fate and fragility of form have never extinguished your love of learning. Thanks for the genes.

I have lived with you in my life and loved you for fifty-one years. I have seen you weak and wounded, strong and stubborn, passive and proactive. There have been times when I have loved you, hated you, been proud of you, been angry with you, felt compassion for you, had respect for you. Life is not consistent and these feelings have waxed and waned over time. But always, I have honored you. You are my father. Your decision gave me life. Your care sustained and protected me when I was young and vulnerable. Your work supported me. That I am, I owe to you completely. Who I am, I owe to you in part. It's a part I mostly like. It's the part that loves books, deeply enjoys and is satisfied by writing, loves music, and respects art.

This week is your eightieth birthday, an appropriate time for reflection and retrospection. As I held up a pair of pants or a file of clippings for you to say keep or toss, I sensed that (not by choice) you were reducing your possessions to a concentrated core. When you kissed your favorite and disintegrating shirt good-bye, I had a sense of how hard this had to have been for you. But I guess I am writing this to tell you that in an unexpected way, I realized today that I am your core. And although I have built myself, there is a part of me that will forever be you. I love you. Happy Birthday, Dad.

Judy

Dear Mom,

I am glad this day has been set aside to remember you, to honor your life and to come to terms with your death. It has been a year and it is right and it is time that I do this.

Let me tell you how I have honored your life in the past year. I have remembered you with love. I have thought about our relationship with each other—what was there as well as what was missing. And I have learned a great deal in the thinking.

I learned how much I miss what used to drive me crazy. I learned how much I missed your warnings when it snowed. I learned that I missed your ten calls a day when I was sick and you wanted to know my temperature. I have come to terms with the fact that I now have a finite number of your afghans. But you taught me how to make them and I taught Amy and so they will continue.

And you will continue. In ways I never imagined, I have come to appreciate new things about you. I appreciate your willingness to face death. You floored me when you said one day, "Do you want to know what I think happens to you when you die?" And when I answered yes, you proceeded to tell me, "I know you'll think this is childish, but I think I will go to heaven and join my parents sitting on a cloud, looking down and watching over you all." I hope so, Mom. I hope so.

After you died, and after the week of mourning, I went back to work. And on a beautiful day at the end of August, I felt overwhelmed by your death and needed to get away from my desk and take a few moments to think about you. I went outside to the picnic table in a small park that abuts my build-

ing and I sat on the table and watched the strong wind make the trees dance against a brilliant blue sky. "Where are you, Mom?" I remember asking as I breathed in the soon-to-be-autumn air. "Where are you?"

And now, as autumn approaches once again, I have my answer. You are in me and Oscar. You are in Paul. You are in Amy. You are in Andy. You are in Den, Pat, Morgan, and Nick. You are in Helen and Morrie. You are in Sam and Ethel. You are in everyone standing here and many who could not be here. I have lived this year without you in my life, but with you in my mind and heart. I honored you during your lifetime and I will continue to honor you during what remains of mine. Thank you for my life and thank you for the lessons I have learned through you. I love you.

Judy

63

"I decided to think about all the bedrooms I had ever had."

MEETING PARENTS AS PEERS

It was a night when I was wired from work, so keyed up that I couldn't sleep. Reading didn't help, TV didn't help. So I took my father's advice. When I was an adolescent and anxious one night, he told me, "You can't think of more than one thing at a time, so sometimes if something is worrying you and you force yourself to think about something else, you find you can relax." That advice is almost forty years old, and it still works.

I used to think about movies I had seen, going through the plots and falling asleep before the end. That didn't work this time either. So I turned off the lights, adjusted the pillows, and decided to think about all the bedrooms I had ever had. Sounds crazy, I know. But my dad was right. As I began to visualize what I could remember of my earliest childhood bedroom, I could see the hollyhocks growing just outside the window. I even remembered getting my first grown-up bed.

I began to relax, but even more amazing to me, I began to think about and appreciate my parents in a new way. I remember my dad padding the headboard of that bed to match the vanity skirt my mother had made. They even made a night table for me out of an old orange crate (I could put my books inside) and draped it in fabric that matched my yellow-and-green-striped curtains. I remembered the huge autumn woodland mural my dad had gotten as a gift from a printing company. He had bordered it with green fabric tape and mounted it on my wall to give me a wider view of the world than was possible from our three-bedroom apartment and my small bedroom window.

I remembered my first desk (elementary school), second desk (high school), and third desk (college) and their places in each of my bedrooms. I remember Dad suggesting that since our closet doors were metal, we could use them as an art gallery. He took us to the museum to select prints and then bought us packets of tiny magnets to hold them up. He encouraged us to make our own art, helping us make spatter prints of leaves with a screen, toothbrush, and colored ink.

As I grew older, my bedrooms came to reflect more of me and less of Mom and Dad. We moved a lot and there were a lot of rooms to remember. Maybe nine or ten. But as I lay in bed in the dark, thinking about those times and those things that had remained in my memory, I also remembered my parents as they had been when I lived in each of those rooms.

And comfort came with the thoughts. Memories emerged like gems being excavated from dark soil. All the hardships of the recent past, of my parents aging into illness, were shoveled aside. And as I dug into my past, along with the memories of my rooms came memories of my parents. But now I was looking back with adult eyes. This was not a child accepting her room as a given. This was a parent looking back at what another parent had done to make a child's room a special place to be. In my reverie I was meeting my parents as peers.

And as my father predicted, along with the memories came relaxation and finally sleep. It was the first time I can remember looking back at my relationship with my parents and exploring not what they said or what they did, but what they created. They had made the limited world of my girlhood bedroom a safe and stimulating place to be, full of books and art and color. And I find myself wondering what other insights will come as I explore what my memory might tell me about them and about myself.

64

"Getting current allowed me to forgive my parents and myself for many things."

WANTING TO LOVE THEM

Most people love their parents—not necessarily all the time, but much of the time. But some people do not, or cannot, love their parents, and suffer terribly from sadness, anger, and guilt. What do we do with disappointments when our parents die? Where do we put these feelings?

When our parents are aging, ill, and dying, they need our help. But how do we help if we have ambivalent feelings about them? How do we help if we've had difficult relationships with them over the years? How do we help if they've become frustrated, angry, stubborn, bitter old people who reject our attempts even when they do love us?

If I said I had the answer, I would be arrogant as well as ignorant. I know just enough to recognize the intricacy of human relations and the enormous complexity that exists between parents and children. But what I can share is the journey I took through that maze of feelings, and the help I got.

Many years before my parents became ill, I recognized that there had been important things missing in our relationship. And what I write about today are the things that *I* missed, not what *they* missed. I'll never know their feelings. But because my parents were human and brought to the table of parenthood their own experiences as children, there were some gaping holes. For my mother, affection was always difficult to express. For my father, anger was impossible to express. As a child, and to this day, I had a great need to feel love as well as to express anger.

And when, in adulthood, I grew to understand the places where our relationship was painful, when I was mature enough to recognize what was missing, I had conflicted feelings. My parents were weakening and beginning to need me, to make demands on me. How would I deal with this new understanding? I couldn't confront them with my anger—they were old, they needed me. I promised myself I wouldn't hurt them. But they were hurting me: when they were self-focused; when they argued with each other and put me in the middle; when, in their suffering, they were unreasonably demanding.

When I looked ahead and saw, based on our relationship, what was coming, I agonized over some of my feelings and decided to seek counseling in an effort to avoid crippling guilt when my parents died. A few years earlier, I had developed a friendship with a family therapist who agreed to set aside time periodically to talk with me about this. At those times, which were professionally focused and different from our social lunches together, I paid her and she listened. We decided on this arrangement so that I could feel free to call when I needed help, and not feel that I was taking advantage of our friendship.

We would meet every few months, when my feelings overwhelmed me and I needed to talk with someone who was not close to the situation. Venting to my friends and family only carried me so far. There were things I wanted and needed to say and consider that could only be said to someone who could offer an objective point of view.

What I learned to recognize over the years was the critical need for me to get and remain "current" with my parents. I struggled to interpret many of the complicated feelings I was having. I worked hard at learning how to share some of them with my parents. And I began to realize that all of them were OK to have.

This didn't mean that I dumped years' worth of resentment and pent-up anger on my parents. What getting current brought me was an understanding of my own feelings (the whys) and some techniques for dealing with my feelings (the hows). So when I arrived on the doorstep of my mother and father's dependence, I was more ready to enter that room.

Caring for aging parents can result in very confusing, mixed, and guilt-producing feelings. It's never too late to ask for help in sorting it all out. I found counseling enormously helpful because it was objective. It wasn't my husband getting angry with my parents when they hurt me. It wasn't my friend getting into the adult-children-dealing-with-aging-parents boat with me. It wasn't my brother rehashing the sore spots of the parenting we received. It was someone unrelated to the situation and uninvolved with the emotional content. It was a fresh pair of eyes, and I began to see more clearly through this new lens.

Getting current allowed me to forgive my parents and myself for many things. It allowed me to be mentally healthy enough to get the job done. It helped me get ready to deal with tough decisions and better manage my powerful feelings. Getting current taught me to think about what I wanted to say to and do for my parents before they died. Much of getting current involved what changed in *my* head, not what I said or did with my parents. It allowed me to show them that I cared when I couldn't tell them. I learned how to be responsible even when I was feeling anger, resentment, and pain. I was better able to speak with them honestly and in a caring way.

I came to recognize that although many people love their parents and have good relationships with them, others do not. But I think everyone *wants* to. Every child, whether young or old, wants to love and be loved by his or her parents. Many may feel a sense of duty and responsibility unconnected to love. That's when it's harder. But good and healthy help can be found in the telephone book (geriatric counseling services), in a county services directory (department of family resources), or in a church, mosque, synagogue, or temple (pastoral counseling).

My experience with the deaths of my parents has taught me the importance of coming to that final bedside with as little left to prove as possible. Then both parties involved can rest in peace.

65

"Things I wanted them to understand before they died."

HARD THINGS TO SAY

Speaking the heart is good for the head. Yesterday my father's best friend fell and broke his hip. And as I stood beside his bed in the emergency room, I had this overwhelming feeling of déjà vu. "I have been here before . . . many times," I thought, as I watched his daughter (*my* best friend) struggle with new feelings in this familiar spot.

That first jolt that our parents really are mortal is sobering and frightening. It can feel very bleak. I remember thinking of all the things I wanted and needed from my parents, and things I dreamt of saying to them before it was too late. And I have written about getting current, learning how to say what I wanted to and needed to. I have also discovered that this doesn't necessarily mean finding an answer or coming to a resolution. Sometimes I could get current by saying things, not solving things. For some problems, there are no solutions.

For me, "current" meant speaking honestly to myself or another person from my mind and from my heart about my situation with my parents and the things I wanted them to understand before they died. It meant sorting out where these feelings came from, and recognizing whether I was dealing with feelings about the present situation or baggage I'd been carrying from the past.

Getting to that place is different for each of us. As I struggled with this issue, I was cautioned by my therapist friend not to judge myself against a perfect standard. She told me to take a step back and look at what I *was* doing for my parents, rather than what I wasn't doing. She reminded me that when your parents are dying, it can feel like an endurance test . . . you get worn down as caretaker. You get tired. It is hard not to feel that you want it to be over and hard not to have guilt about that feeling. But that is a normal and very human feeling.

Walking that final mile with our parents involves others, not just our parents and ourselves. And it can be just as tough to communicate with them during this difficult time. So I have made a list of the things I tried to say and show to the people I love.

To my parents:

I love you.

This is very hard but I am doing it because of my feelings for you.

It is how I honor you.

It makes me angry when you . . .

It makes it harder for me when you . . .

I feel guilty when you . . .

I feel sad when . . .

If you won't do it for yourself, please do it for me (use your walker).

I will miss you when . . .

Don't worry, I will take care of Mom/Dad when you are gone.

Are you afraid to die?
Do you want to talk about death?
What is worrying you?
Are you afraid of hurting me?
I am afraid of hurting you.
I know you tried to be the best parent you could be.
You did a good job.
I appreciate all you did for me.
I am proud of you.
I will always remember . . .
I forgive you for your mistakes with me.
I hope you will forgive my mistakes with you.
I know we weren't as close as we might have wished in the past, but there is the here and now to work in.
Thank you for my life.

To my husband:

I love you.
I need your support and understanding.
I cannot always tell you what I need because this situation is so complex, so please understand that sometimes when I am angry, it is not with you and that sometimes I don't know what I need or whom I'm angry with.
I appreciate your love and help more than I can tell you.
I know you get angry sometimes with me and/or my parents and that's OK. You are entitled to feel your feelings despite this situation.

I know you often feel neglected, but this is temporary and I will try as hard as I can to maintain some sense of balance in our lives while this lasts.

Despite my preoccupation with my parents, you are very important to me.

I am so grateful that we are in this together, that I am not alone.

Please forgive me when I "lose it."

Please understand how hard this is for me.

I know that when my parents hurt me, it hurts you too.

I know that they do things that hurt you.

Please let me vent.

Please help me make decisions.

I need to cry.

Touching helps, please hug me.

Tell me what *you* need.

I know this is hurting you too.

I feel loved when . . .

Thank you for loving me through this.

To my grown children:

I love you.

You are important to me.

I am frustrated when I can't be available to you because of this.

It's OK when you get angry with Grandma or Grandpa.

Your relationship with them belongs to you and them, not to me. I won't tell you what you should do.

It's OK to be afraid or repulsed by what you may see and hear at the nursing home or hospital.

It's OK not to enjoy visiting them when they are ill and angry.

Death is a natural part of life.

I appreciate your help.

I value your opinions.

I am modeling the way I would like to be treated when I am old and frail.

We are not obligated to love one another. Love is interactive.

I appreciate it when you comfort me.

I feel loved when . . .

You have helped me struggle through this.

We are doing this hard thing as a family.

I get angry sometimes with what I have to do and I want you to understand that I am not angry with you.

I hope I can spare you much of this pain when I get old and frail.

You are their legacy and mine.

To my brother:

I love you.

Regardless of who does what for Mom and Dad, we are equal partners in the decision-making.

This is not a contest.

I know this is hurting you.

I hope we can work as a team.

I value your opinion.

I respect your advice.

I want us to share the responsibilities.

I also want us to share the consequences of any decisions we make.

I want to consider all the options we both can think of before we make a decision.

What do you need from me?

What do you want from me?

How can I help you?

Here's how you can help me . . .

I'm glad that we can go through this together rather than alone.

It makes me angry when . . .

I recognize that we have different relationships with Mom and Dad and different feelings about them.

I think I understand how you feel about Mom and Dad.

I think you understand how I feel about Mom and Dad.

How can we help them without hurting our relationship?

For me, this process involved speaking, showing, writing, anything I could think of to get my message across and to help hear theirs. Sometimes it was conscious and sometimes not. I tried to remember that people couldn't read my mind; I had to tell them my thoughts and needs. Most of all, I had to remind myself that while I was trying to help my parents, it was important to help myself as well. Getting current is hard work. I tried to remember that although the goal was important to me, if I couldn't do it with my parents, with my husband, with my children, or with my brother, it was critical to become current with myself.

PART V

Morning

Survival

The dawn gives way to morning and feelings of survival stretch for the sunlight. Pleasure begins to return when I remember my parents. The joy of memory is no longer always tinged with sadness. But I recognize that among these tender shoots, the weeds of pain still have their roots. I cultivate my garden carefully.

Closure continues to come in measured steps. Pain diminishes and is sometimes replaced by new understanding. Regret is fading, and unhappy memories are becoming less powerful. Reflection often brings comfort instead of remorse as I recognize and consciously think about the good things that have come of this journey with my parents.

Very slowly, I begin to discard the useless baggage I have been carrying in my home, in my head, and in my heart. And much to my surprise, the empty spaces are filling with satisfaction and pleasure. A very long and hard journey is behind me. Life without my parents beckons. I gather the things they gave me, the lessons I have learned, and the love we shared, and I set out into the future strengthened by the experience. I am beginning to feel whole again.

66

"My father left me his books,
and with them come pleasure and pain."

LEGACIES

I held the book in my hand and smelled my father. In the murky light of my garage, standing before the cartons of other books yet uncrated that my father left me, I withdrew this one to give to my father's friend and revisited a lifetime of memories about my father and his books.

From the time I can first remember, my father loved his books third—after his wife and his children. He had begun collecting them as a child, and each was the precious friend of a man who had been a lonely and introverted boy. If we are known by the society of our friends, then my father was in good company: Emerson, Thoreau, James, Stevenson. To this day I can describe the covers, if not the contents, of each book. The dark green, soft leather-bound copy of *Walden* with gold wavy stripes along the spine, the half-size red set of the works of Robert Louis Stevenson, with gold lettering.

Dad's collection represented the unique love affair he had with information. As a man who would better have spent his life in a college classroom, but who chose instead to make his living in retail business, he never had time for close friendships with the minds he so revered. Instead he settled for passing acquaintanceship, feeling satisfied enough just to be in their company. He had completely read only selections of the more than a thousand books he owned by the time he died. But he had tasted almost all of them. Working from nine until nine left very little energy to bring to reading. And so he was very selective about what he dipped into, reserving those priceless minutes of his middle age for reading about modern art, philosophy, and science.

But he took special pride in knowing exactly where each book lived on the shelves scattered throughout the many places he and my mother called home. I can remember his boasting that there wasn't a subject we could name that he couldn't find some reference on in his library. And my brother and I came to believe him when, in junior high school, my brother needed information on professional boxing and my father had a book.

Always a bit awkward with people, my father interacted with his books in an almost spiritual way. We have a photograph of my dad holding me when I was only a few months old. He is tentative, as if he is afraid he'll drop me. As if I were fragile and a little frightening. But he never touched a book without caressing it. He loved his books with his hands, his eyes, and his mind. And although he would spend his last cent on a book, my father never put his name in one because he felt it was profane to own a book. "Books belong to the world," I remember him telling me. No one really owns a book. And so, with the exception of a few books from his early youth, when he had experimented with the feeling of using bookplates, his books remained anonymously possessed.

My father was a good provider. His books lived on revered shelves and were ceremoniously vacuumed once a year at my mother's insistence. I really think he loved taking them out one at a time and dusting off his treasures. He recruited my brother and me to help with this chore as a way of introducing us to his favorite writers. The match took and he ignited in us a love and respect for the written word. He used to give us lessons on how to open a new book so as not to injure its spine. We came to appreciate the heft of a book, the texture of its paper, the feel of its binding, the smell of its ink.

And so when, today, I decided to send one of his books to his best friend as a memory of my father, I found myself plunged into a sea of memories. I thought about the poems he read to me, the ideas he shared with me from his readings, and the books he gave my family over the years as gifts.

Our parents leave us many legacies. Legacies of pleasure, legacies of pain. They leave us joys and wounds. They leave us things and feelings. They leave us ideas and examples. My father left me his books. And with them come all those other things.

67

"Reluctantly releasing my mother's handwritten note to the trash can, I kissed it good-bye."

BALANCING THE BOOKS

I leaned into the pain. It was old and familiar: the stomach knot, the band of tension above the eyes, the dry mouth. Before me on the kitchen table lay the final vestiges of my parents' lives. And I discovered that in closing out their accounts and finishing up their final paperwork, I was opening doors I thought I had locked forever.

Two checks I had written in the months after their deaths had never been cashed, and now it was time to follow through and straighten out any errors. It had been a long, slow climb to the place of comfort I had finally found. Months and months of untangling nerves that had been twisted and jangled by the decision to remove my parents from life support. But comfort fled in the face of memories.

Tracking back through the notebooks of records I had so meticulously kept, I again faced their medications, their surgeries, their losses. But there were other accounts as well, accounts of the minutiae of their lives: homeowners insurance policies that went back to the 1970s on homes and apartments long since vacated, birth certificates, death certificates, notes they had written and stored carefully in their small, gray, metal fireproof box. I stopped and read these papers that I had handled so thoughtlessly before, as I had crammed responsibility for their lives into the overextended moments of my own.

As I searched for errors and made corrections in the paperwork, I recognized that it was finally time to throw away the long-extinct policies and the now meaningless notes. And yet . . . and yet, I was not prepared for the powerful emotions that accompanied the task. My mother had written "safety deposit box" on a small slip of white paper. Reluctantly releasing it to the trash can, I kissed it good-bye. Her handwriting is still as familiar to me as my own. My father had written notes on the paperwork for their cemetery plots. I silently thanked him for his forethought and pressed the paper to my lips before throwing it away.

Then I came to an envelope marked "certificates" that contained both of my parents' birth certificates. I had read them before with eyes hungry to satisfy social security requirements and the demands for death certificate information. Those readings had been frantic and intense searches to meet deadlines. This time I read them out of curiosity. I was surprised to notice that my mother's parents had been twenty-eight and twenty-five—old for the times—when she was born, the middle child of three; and my father's parents had been a tender twenty-one and twenty when he was born, the second child of five. Dad's parents had been so young. Both of my parents had been born at home, delivered by midwives. Why had I not known that?

As the pile in the trash can grew, the pile in the fireproof box was reduced to a concentrated core of memorabilia and vital statistics that were no longer vital. I gathered together the information I would need to bring final closure to their medical accounts and their checking accounts. As I placed the necessary forms in my Day Runner to take to work, I felt guilty that it had taken me so long to gather the will to revisit these papers. I would call the bank tomorrow about the uncashed checks. But tonight, in the quiet of my family room, as I packed all the notebooks into a carton marked "Mom and Dad Records," I was visiting another kind of bank . . . a memory bank. It was a hard visit. But after tomorrow, all accounts would finally be paid—in many ways.

68

"I can't tell my mother, so I'm telling you."

NOT SHARING GOOD NEWS

I called my mother's best friend with the news. It was a joyous family event, and I wanted her to know. She answered and I blurted out, "Helen! My brother just became a grandfather and I can't tell my mother, so I'm telling you." There was a pause before Helen spoke, and I felt the tears coming. We were both missing my mom.

These feelings sneak up on me at very odd and unexpected times. When it snows. Driving to work. When good news happens. For a mother and daughter who struggled mightily to become closer, and never really made it until just before she died, Mom and I are bound by past and future memories in ways I never would have imagined.

My mother was a disappointed woman for a good part of her life . . . and it embarrasses me to say that I never really knew what she wanted so I never really understood all the things that may have disappointed her. She didn't talk to me much about her dreams and ambitions. But in her own way, she let me know that I was not a disappointment.

Her celebrations were reined in by her predisposition to worry. I became so used to the, "That's wonderful, but . . ." that I braced myself in advance even when I was telling her something that was very good. I thought of that when I shared the news about Jordan Elizabeth's birth with Helen. That's the kind of sneaky remembering that threads its way into my life without my mother. She would have rejoiced, I know, at the birth of her grandson's daughter. She would have had a handmade afghan and bunting ready, would have talked excitedly with my brother, and would have confided all her joy and worry to Helen. And in two months, another grandson, my son, will marry, and I will miss sharing the event with my mother. That's the future memory I was talking about, the first of hundreds of happy things that I anticipate and cannot share with her.

Ours was a sweet-and-sour love affair. I know she loved me. And looking back, I recognize that I loved her and told her so. She just could never clearly say that to me. Sometimes, I think, it's very hard to quantify and define love. There were times when I really wondered if I loved her . . . when she was so negative, when she was unresponsive. But since she's been gone, I find myself comforted by missing her. It is a confirmation of the meaningful place she held in my life.

And so, when I visit New Orleans this month on a business trip, I will take with me the last of the baby buntings my mother made and give it to Jordan. It's a wonderful way to share this family event with the woman who raised me, who loved me, and who left me lessons (good and bad) that are part of who I am. Even more important, it is a way to share this woman who would have loved her—with Jordan.

69

"The fragile-looking bent-over old man looked and moved just like my father."

BEING WITH DAD AGAIN

I am engulfed by a spasm of grief. I saw him in produce and my heart stopped. I followed him into dairy in disbelief. There, in my local supermarket, in the middle of everyone's ordinary life, I saw my father again. Same hat. Same jacket. Same shoes. Same haircut. Same walk. Same silver stubble. Waves of longing washed over me as I worked through my shopping list. The fragile-looking bent-over old man looked and moved just like my father.

It was late and I was on my way home with dinner, but I found myself walking the aisles one final time, just to catch a glimpse of him. I found him again, and again my heart caught.

I got on line to check out, struggling to control the feelings of loss that had so surprised me. The old gentleman got in line several checkers down and my eyes were drawn to him as if he were magnetic. I kept trying to look away, but couldn't. And then to my dismay, he came over and got in line behind me. He only had three or four things in his cart, so I invited him to get in front of me. He thanked me, and we spoke for a few moments. It was astonishing. He even sounded like my father, the low, barely audible, somewhat courtly rumble I will never forget. Every detail of his appearance is burned into my mind. The way his white hair curled over his neck, the way his hands were bent, the way his fingernails looked.

He paid for his groceries with the same drawn-out gestures I remember so well, taking his money from his wallet almost in slow motion. Then he pushed his cart out of the store, shuffling behind it, and left me crying at the checkout counter. The young cashier was either oblivious to my tears, or she very kindly chose not to notice. For one of the few times I can remember, I was totally unable to control myself. I daubed my eyes as I wrote my check, still unable to stop the flow of sorrow and memory.

And outside the store, there he was again, obviously worried and waiting for something or somebody. I thought he might need help, so I approached and asked. He explained that he was fine, only waiting for his daughter who was still shopping in the store. And he apologized for moving ahead of me in line. With purpose, I placed my hand on his arm and told him it had been a pleasure to talk with him because he reminded me of my father. I remember wanting to touch him.

I cried all the way home, missing my father as never before. I sat in my driveway, weeping beside my bags of groceries. And as I got out of the car and noticed that the branches of the tree in front of my house had begun to thicken with buds, I remembered my father's words again, "Some day spring will come and I won't be here, but you will. . . . And that's as it should be." He had prepared me, in a special way, to miss him. But he had had no way to prepare me for the overwhelming feelings that tell us how much we still love someone who has died. He had tried to prepare me for his death and for living without him. But he had not been able to prepare me for the pleasure and the pain of remembering him.

70

"Your mind and body get used to being taut."

FEELING GRIEF AND RELIEF

Sitting in the beautiful sanctuary with my future daughter-in-law Dana on Easter Sunday morning, I marveled at the sunlight streaming through the trees that surrounded the church. The rays of light marked the room with patterns that danced quietly across the walls. The lush colors of the flowers and the life sounds of the silent congregation were peaceful. A baby cried out and people shifted in their seats as the service began.

The children of the congregation shared flowers with each worshiper, and the minister recounted the historical and spiritual significance of the season and the day. As he spoke poignantly of life and death, I found myself remembering my parents. And the numbing relief that I had failed to recognize since their deaths dissolved suddenly and unexpectedly into a flood of grief.

"Why cry now?" I thought, dabbing at my eyes with a sodden tissue. I had grieved with Mom and Dad for two years before they died, as I saw them struggle not to lose themselves in the agony of their illnesses. And I have grieved for more than a year and a half since their deaths. But I realized that this was a new kind of pain, very different from before. Dana turned to me questioningly, and I could only catch my breath enough to say that I was remembering my parents. With touching compassion, she put her arm around me, kissed me, and sat with me as I wept.

Fast-forward a week: I am lunching with two of my fiftyish-year-old friends and recounting this experience. Between the three of us, five parents have died and the sixth is now suffering greatly. It surprises me to discover that both my friends understand exactly what I am talking about. "You know," I think aloud, "when someone you love suffers long and hard before they die there is a period of pure relief that you feel when it is over . . . for them and for yourself." They nod. "And maybe," I continue, "the relief you feel delays your ability to really grieve." More nods. "I wonder if you can feel relief and grief at the same time?"

The question hangs in the air for several moments. Then we all agree that identifying what grief feels like is very difficult because guilt, relief, exhaustion, and pain get in the way. And they can last a long, long time.

Today, speaking with my friend who has been watching her mother suffer for several years, we decided that when you're dealing with this kind of agony, you steel yourself daily to deal with the awful moments. And after years of bracing yourself against the pain and fear, of preparing for the loss, your mind and body get used to being taut. Coming down from that can take a long time.

For me it was a journey I was making unaware. The pain is no longer fresh. Scar tissue has formed. But it is only now that I have begun to realize the strength and depth of this experience. Now that time has passed and I am no longer braced, I can feel more of my feelings, and I understand better what accompanies the loss of a parent. Though I think that I still have much more to learn.

71

"I watched the teller erase my parents and their paper persona from the bank's files."

CLOSING ACCOUNTS

I had been to this bank hundreds of times before they died: with my mother, with my father, with my notebooks as I tried to help them manage their finances. This time it was different. I stood at the teller's window with my memories, closing their accounts and closing the door to my responsibilities to my parents.

Explaining to the young teller that I wanted to close the checking accounts I had established for my parents, I fought for control. With empathy, the young man said, "Your parents are deceased?" I nodded and he proceeded with the everyday, mundane paperwork that erased my parents and their paper persona from the bank's active files.

It had taken me nineteen months to be able to do this. Nineteen months of paying final bills, checking final records. I had procrastinated beyond what was conscionable. I wanted this, but I dreaded it. I wanted to be finished with the record-keeping, to pack away the dozen white notebooks I had used to keep track of their affairs, to put the important papers that were no longer important down in my basement. But there was a part of me that worried that putting their papers out of my life might mean putting my parents in the same place. Stupid, I know. But feelings work this way sometimes. The mind knows, and the feelings feel, and sometimes the connection goes awry.

With my husband standing beside me, his arm on my shoulder, I went through this rite of passage, emerging from the bank finally responsible only for my own affairs. No medical worries about my parents. No financial worries. No meeting-the-requirements-of-the-Medicaid-law worries. No insurance worries. No nursing home worries. No Social Security worries. It was the end of record-keeping . . . and the beginning of memory-keeping.

There is no longer a corner of my desk devoted to the piles of mail and bank statements they continued to receive even after they died. The pile reminded me of them always, and of the responsibility I still had to them. Now, when I remember them, the memories will spring from other sources.

It is one of many closures I have experienced since my parents died. And along with the sadness of this particular closure also comes satisfaction. This was the end of the final miles I had promised myself I would walk with Mom and Dad. And when the teller stamped "account closed" on their papers, I was stamping the same on my mind and heart. Bills paid. Job done. Promises kept.

72

"There are better things to remember them by."

RELEASING THE RECORDS

"They're dead, hon," my husband said. And even with the kindness in his eyes, the phrase sent a cold chill through my body. It sounded so final. It *was* so final. We had been talking about cleaning our basement and I had just mentioned that I didn't know what to do with the three cartons of my parents' papers. I had been saving them since Mom and Dad died more than two years ago. They were records of bills I had paid, correspondence I had handled, bank records I had reconciled.

"Throw them away," my husband suggested, and I sat thinking about doing just that . . . putting those boxes in the trash. There was a part of me that wanted to keep the connection and a part of me that wanted to be rid of those painful reminders of endless hours of frustration and agony. In a very visceral way, those pieces of paper were a connection to my parents, to their final years, to the journey we had made together into their old age, illnesses, and deaths.

I didn't trust my instincts, so I called a friend who was a lawyer. "You can get rid of them," he advised. "Your parents left no property; no one is going to come after you." He was right about the property. And yet I have a wonderful legacy from my parents. I have their books. I have their photograph albums. I have the things they made for us over the years, the knitted blankets and sweaters, the scrapbooks.

I called my brother for his opinion. "Toss them," he agreed. "There are better things to remember them by." So I went downstairs to the boxes carefully marked "Mom and Dad's financial records." They were heavy, filled with the white notebooks in which I used to keep track of everything. So many memories. This truly was the final reminder of all my work.

Closure seems to come in spurts, spread out over the years since my parents died. I have the sense I'm still not finished . . . that I will never be finished. It was very hard for me to pay those final bills. It was very hard for me to close out the accounts they had. It was hard to notify all the agencies that needed to know: Social Security, Medicaid, Medicare, Blue Cross Blue Shield. And now it's hard for me to separate myself from the confirmation that I carried out all those responsibilities.

Resolving to move forward, I emptied each carton, paged

through each notebook, and said good-bye to my meticulous lists documenting their monthly phone bills, nursing-home payments, and saved receipts. I carried the resulting trash bags to the backyard, breathless because they were so heavy. And then I called my brother on the phone and cried.

Letting go comes to us in many guises. I had not even realized that I was still holding on. I have the hope and the sense that throwing away those records will be a bit freeing. I remind myself that I am letting go of the papers, and some of the pain, but not of the past. The trash will be picked up seven days from today, and the bags are in the yard even as I type, black and shiny, wet with winter rain. It is time, I think, to make room in my basement and in my life for other things.

73

"I wish I had touched my parents more when they were old."

SPEAKING WITHOUT WORDS

I should have touched my parents more. Skin is a wonderful translator when we cannot speak. I think that we often save touching for our most intense moments. At funerals we grasp the mourners and struggle for appropriate words. At weddings we throw our arms around the bride and groom and hold tight in the delight of shared joy. We welcome loved ones at airports with open arms. At graduations, overwhelmed by pride, we caress our children. Our deepest feelings, often difficult to articulate, find expression as we reach out to touch someone. But ordinary moments can be powerful opportunities.

I wish I had touched my parents more when they were old. I think that touching may have been difficult for them to initiate; they were not touchy-feely people. But I think they may have enjoyed being on the receiving end, and it never occurred to me that I might have done more of it until last night when it was almost two years too late.

Lying in bed after midnight at the end of a holiday weekend, I was reading a series of magazine articles about the human senses. I plowed through "taste" and learned a great deal. I read "smell" and chuckled at some of the explanations I recognized (like why I can't taste a thing when I have a cold). And then I came to "touch." The article talked about how gentle massaging has a soothing effect on premature babies and babies born with their mother's drug addiction. It dealt with helping autistic children become accustomed to touching others and tolerating others touching them. I read about how single men and women can often feel "touch deprived," and how sometimes massage can help calm a person with Alzheimer's disease who becomes agitated.

Ker-chunk! Another piece of the puzzle fell into place as I realized that many of the things I had difficulty saying to my parents might have been communicated in another way. As they became old and ill, it was sometimes hard just to say, "I love you," because it felt as if I were saying good-bye. I didn't want to frighten them, and I didn't want to frighten myself. But I might have sat and held their hands. I might have talked and stroked their arms. I might have put my arm around them while we talked.

Sometimes, when I was wheeling my Dad around in his wheelchair, I would pat the bald spot on the top of his head, or lean down and kiss it. Sometimes I would wheel my mother around and put my hand on her shoulder. I can remember how thin and bony she felt to me. I think that when age and illness rob people of their familiar physique, we sometimes hesitate to touch what has become an uncomfortable reminder of mortality and loss. My father had had a stroke and half of his body was numb. My mother had neuropathy and felt nothing through her hands and feet. Did they miss touching? Did they miss feeling touched?

I thought about touching for a long time before I could fall asleep. And this morning, I shared my thoughts with a close friend whose aging mother is desperately ill and mostly unaware. "You know," she said, "it's funny you should mention that today. Just this weekend, my sister flew into town and when we visited Mom, I noticed that as my sister sat next to her, stroking her forehead, my mother seemed to relax and respond."

Many of us, I think, do not speak this language with ease. And yet it is one of the most primal forms of communication and connection. Perhaps the Puritan ethic Americans often practice gets in the way. As our intellect develops, we find speech and hearing and vision to be the tools of choice for communication. Often we reserve touching for passion, for anger, for those explosive feelings we cannot easily contain.

We love the very young with our hands. We press them

to us and they cling in sweet and inarticulate dependence. We stroke the animals we love who do not speak our language: our cats, our dogs, our horses. We touch them to let them know we care, and they respond with their own bodies, moving next to us, touching us back. And so, I am thinking that for those of us who feel deeply and struggle to find the right words, for those of us who may have had a less than perfect communication with our parents, for those of us who may feel overwhelmed by impending loss, or who find it difficult at the end of life to say what we want to . . . perhaps there is another way.

74

"The pain came and went like waves
beating against the shore, and I surfed the surges."

THE ANNIVERSARY OF MOM'S DEATH

The date snuck up on me and made me lonely. Suddenly, in the midst of everyday life—cooking dinner, meeting work deadlines, spending a weekend with one of my children at his home—comes the day my mother died. I hadn't thought about it much until it happened, until it intruded on the quiet of my mind and wouldn't go away. Exactly two years ago yesterday I took my mother off life support, and according to what I believe on paper and in her heart were her wishes, I helped her to die.

It was the first thing I thought about as I woke up. It lingered as I did my morning exercises. Listening to the news on the drive to work didn't help me forget. I got to my desk and dove into the pile of mail that had accumulated. And in a twist of fate I can only shake my head and wonder at, I unfolded a thick newsletter from the American Psychological Association to find a front-page article on end-of-life decisions.

Reading the article, I felt immeasurably sad and enormously grateful. Sad at the scenes that kept popping into my mind like slides running through a projector. Grateful that this issue was getting the attention it deserves. And the morning wore on slowly. The article made me cry and I closed my office door to have the privacy to feel my feelings. I called my best friend to see if we could meet for lunch, not sharing my anguish but feeling reassured by her voice. She had a repairman coming, though, could we meet next week? I hung up, still feeling empty.

Waffling about whether or not to call my brother and stir up his memories of that day we shared so intensely, I gave into the pain and phoned him at work. I could tell by his hello that it was one of his "nutsy" days, one of those days when he was stretched to the limit trying to meet deadlines. So I didn't say why I had called and we agreed to talk later in the evening.

More tears came, and rather than fight them, I sat at my desk thinking about my mom, about how she looked that day, about how I felt that day, about who she was, about who I had become since she died. The pain came and went like waves beating against the shore, and I surfed the surges.

Then I phoned my husband at his office. He's really wonderful about stopping his day and listening to me when I need it. We spoke as I sipped my cup of cooling coffee and he helped me as he has so many other times when I have been hurting. Swallowing the huge lump in my throat, I explained that what I thought I needed was processing time, and my work today wasn't going to allow me that. "We'll talk more together this evening," he promised, and I felt better.

There was no one else I could call who would understand. As I had on the day Mom died, I felt alone with what was in my mind and in my heart. And so with reverence for the powerful feelings that accompany the dying process, I pushed the thoughts and memories aside, having given them what I thought was their due for the day. And with much effort, I moved on to the responsibilities of my work.

What I learned from the day is that I probably will never really finish saying good-bye to my parents. Eight weeks from now, I will go through this again on the anniversary of my father's death. "It's OK," I remind myself. "It's to be expected. It's part of the process of grieving." And as I opened my office door, the phone rang. It was someone who needed help for a child who has a disability. I got to work, trading my pain for hers. Tucking my mother into a corner of my mind, I moved further into my life without her.

75

"Why don't I remember those kinds of moments with my mom?"

THE LEGACY OF LETTERS

As soon as I drew the envelope out of the old shoe box and saw the 1960 New Jersey postmark, I knew that the letter was from my mother. It had been typed on her old mechanical Royal typewriter and the news was thirty-eight years old. Fingering the yellowed envelope, I wondered what it would feel like to read it again and hear her voice in my head. I began the first of two carefully typed pages. In the summer of 1960 I had been a college intern working in Washington. Mom was writing from New Jersey where she and Dad had recently moved after more than twenty years in D.C.

The letter was newsy, filling me in on family happenings, and full of the daily routine of her life. She observed. She reported. She advised. The letter was Mom-familiar . . . until I got to the middle, where several innocent lines jumped off the page. "When you get home, we'll go on a shopping spree and outfit you from the inside out, starting with all new underwear. I'm saving my money and looking forward to it." I could not remember doing that kind of mother-daughter thing with my mom.

The fact that I didn't remember stuck in my mind. Why don't I remember those kinds of moments with my mom?

Were they too ordinary? When I was nineteen and she, forty-seven, had I missed the enthusiasm, the anticipation, and the pleasure in her letter? Now that I'm almost fifty-seven, I'm meeting her as a peer through these letters. Now that I'm a mother, I know what she was talking about; I can decode the message. How many times do mothers and daughters speak different languages to each other?

After letting regret simmer on the back burners of my mind for a whole week, I came to a new insight about my mother and me. The rigidity, routine, and control that governed her life, which I railed against for so many years, may have cast a shadow over our relationship that obscured some really good things, like shopping, cooking, and crocheting together.

I think memory tends to preserve our powerful feelings while the ordinary, everyday, comfortable ones seem to meld into the background. Perhaps our everyday feelings are written in the invisible ink that only emerges when placed above a flame. Mom's death seared me and I wept bitterly for what never was between us. But maybe there was more than I thought. I find that the few letters my mother wrote to the young-adult me are very nourishing to the middle-aged woman I have become.

In life we seemed to speak to each other in coded messages that neither of us clearly understood. Her letters have provided a key to understanding what she was saying all along. In the midst of her routine and rigidity, in the midst of my struggle to separate from her, we really did love one another.

76

". . . I remembered the view from those two windows which became my parents' lens on life . . ."

LOOKING IN AND OUT

I've driven by hundreds of times without looking up, but this time, for some reason, my eyes traveled to the eighth floor and found the windows. And unexpectedly, I felt a lump in my throat as I remembered what had been there. I was looking at the windows of my parents' old apartment. For the last ten years of their lives, before they moved into the nursing home, Mom and Dad had shared a living room, one small bedroom, a bathroom, and a tiny galley kitchen so small that only one person at a time could fit in.

"They're just windows," I thought, wiping away the tears. But in the seconds it took me to drive by, I remembered every single thing about that apartment. It's almost like remembering my parents, thinking about how well I knew their faces, their hands, their expressions. And pulling into the parking lot of my office, I sat in the car for a few minutes, picturing my parents' last home, visualizing each piece of furniture, each knickknack, the afghans on each bed, the paintings on the walls, the photographs of the kids cluttering each flat surface. I remembered the curtains, the carpet, the dishes, the way the front door groaned when you opened it.

I also remembered the view from those two windows,

which became my parents' lens on life for so many years, as getting outside became more and more difficult for them. Looking into those windows had reminded me of what I had seen looking out of those windows. The snowy days when the city beneath them was covered in white. The summer days when the haze of humidity hung so heavily in the air that nearby buildings looked almost impressionistic.

I remembered the light my mother always kept on over the sink in the pink kitchen. And the books, the final precious few that my father had tucked into every corner of that small space. The books were *his* window on the world. They had always given him access to the places he would dream about but never see. They expanded his world far beyond the space in which he lived.

I thought about the thousands of times I had ridden the elevator up to that apartment, to bring the kids, to bring groceries, to bring help. I thought of the three closets crammed with the detritus of eighty years of life: the old vacuum cleaner, my father's hats, the slide projector, the collection of old towels that could tell stories of my childhood if they spoke. I thought about the blinds on the windows, grimy with the residue of life without spring cleaning. My mother's homes had always been spotless. Whistle clean. But that had disappeared when the aches and pains of old age had arrived. And much to my surprise, Mom had given in and mellowed enough to tolerate a less than immaculate home. . . . But maybe she hadn't given in. Maybe she had just endured.

It was time to return to the office. "Is it just me?" I wondered, getting out of the car. I felt as if I were emerging from a time capsule. "Why is it that our parents' final homes are so etched in our minds?" I wondered, as I made my way into my building. "Because they are our final history with our mothers and fathers? Because they are the last residue of our childhood homes? Because ancient, faded towels *do* talk and old vacuum cleaners *are* artifacts?" Proust had it right in *Remembrance of Things Past;* seemingly insignificant objects *can* evoke feelings, smells, visions of what used to be.

Those two windows, high on the eighth floor of a senior citizens' apartment building in Rockville, Maryland, have voices of their own. They speak directly to me every time I drive by and look at them. They are my final connection with my first home.

77

"I have learned that I am stronger than I thought."

LESSONS

When my three children were little, every time we took a trip we asked them to keep a journal. It was hard to get them to do it sometimes, but at the end of each day they would write a few lines in a spiral notebook about what they had done or how they felt. Today, these books are among their most prized possessions. Replete with spelling and grammatical errors, their childish scrawl broken by smears of erasure marks, these journals are a record of what they thought and how they felt during our journeys as a family. Each is a book of memories, calling up what it felt like to be seven camping in North Carolina, or ten visiting Disney World, or twelve flying to California. Each is a summary of what they thought was important and what they had learned in each day.

So too is this journal of my journey with my parents into their old age a summary of how I have felt and what I have learned. And I thought that it might be useful for me to spend some time looking back, gathering together the lessons I have learned.

About feelings, I have learned:

. . . that I am stronger than I thought.

. . . that I can do very hard things.

. . . that I really did love my parents (sometimes I wondered).

. . . that I have to learn to ask for what I need (my family can't read my mind).

. . . that it's OK to have needs (I am not Superwoman).

. . . that families carry much baggage on their journey together (anger, resentment, hurt feelings).

. . . that I desperately wanted to hear my mother and father say that they loved me before they died, even though I am fifty-five and know that they did.

. . . that it was important for me to tell them that I loved them before they died.

. . . that humor can reside in unexpected places (bringing my mother her repaired teeth for Mother's Day).

. . . that anger needs to be vented before it builds to an eruption.

. . . that eruptions don't always mean yelling and screaming. Eruptions can be migraines, your body's way of saying, "I can't handle any more. Enough."

. . . that it is important for me to listen to the messages my body is sending.

. . . that it's OK to have all kinds of "bad" feelings. It's what I do and how I act upon those feelings that matters.

. . . that it's normal to want my parents' suffering and my suffering to end, and that I don't have to feel guilty about it.

. . . that my brother and I had to work hard to keep together during this time (we didn't always make it).

. . . that my husband and children love me enough to work at understanding how this responsibility affected my life.

. . . that there is nothing as comforting as the love and caring of good people (whether they are family, friends, coworkers, or complete strangers).

From my parents, I have learned:

. . . that they were not afraid to look at death, or to talk about it, not afraid to help me prepare for theirs and ultimately for my own.

. . . that amidst the self-focus that increased with their descent into frailty, they did love me.

. . . that they were full and complete people—with

rich histories and childhood, adolescent, and adult identities of their own—not solely parents.

. . . that I value parts of their legacy (love of books, ability to crochet, appreciation of art, enjoyment of reading, organizational skills, practicality, respect for hard work, commitment to honesty).

. . . that some of what they left me was not healthy (fear of new things, the goal of perfection, the tendency to worry too much, the need for reassurance that people love me, the difficulty dealing with anger).

. . . that it takes courage to grow old.

From my husband and children, I have learned:

. . . that being supportive is a learned skill (they learned how and practiced it).

. . . that listening is powerful medicine. When they listened to my anger, my pain, my sadness, and my fear, they shared the burden and strengthened my ability to continue with the task.

. . . that my children have grown into adults whose opinions I value, whose advice I respect, and whose understanding I appreciate. Many of my moments of clearest understanding about my parents came out of discussions with my children and the honesty of their sharing.

. . . that working together is not a constant; it waxes and wanes, and this is normal and OK.

. . . that we can recover from our disagreements

when we love each other enough to be willing to work at it.

. . . that love comes in many forms, and some people show it better by their actions than by their words.

. . . that touching is an important way to communicate what often is difficult to say.

. . . that touching can bring comfort and strength.

. . . that it is OK to need help and important to ask for it.

. . . that some problems need saying, not solving.

From my friends, I have learned:

. . . that most of us have experienced or will experience the death of our parents and that we can learn from and help each other.

. . . that speaking our minds and hearts to another person is cathartic and therapeutic.

. . . that the unconditional acceptance and safety of friendship is a refuge and a comfort.

. . . that in an honest exchange of ideas with people we respect and trust, we often find permission to feel our feelings, without guilt, and that this is a gift.

From myself, I have learned:

. . . that I have skills I was unaware of.

. . . that it is important to recognize my feelings for what they are (to be able to identify anger when I feel it, guilt when I feel it, fear when I feel it, grief when I feel it, sadness when I feel it).

... that not all grief feels sad. Some of it can feel like confusion, inability to focus, exhaustion, or physical pain.

... that in middle age, I can continue to learn and grow.

... that what doesn't kill me will make me stronger.

... that humor is a life preserver.

... that I will die and that I can live with this understanding and prepare for it.

From my readers, I am learning:

... that I am not alone on this journey.

78

"Writing has been good medicine for me."

FEARS, FEELINGS, AND THE FLOW OF TIME

When my parents died, I was assaulted by my feelings. Ripped apart by decisions I was called on to make. Pounded by regrets. Torn by anger. Aching with loss. Terrified of my own mortality. Most of all, I was afraid that I might forget them if they were not in my life. Like mountains, these once young and jagged emotions have become older, rounded, and less raw with the passage of time. Their power has shifted from stark and sharp to softer and smoother. It was not an easy passage, but the questions that threatened me then are slowly being answered.

Would I feel guilty about implementing my parents' advance directives, following their wishes, and removing them from life support? So far, the answer is no. I think often about those two decisions. And I have indelible memories of the days that followed taking my mother off medication and removing my father from dialysis. But my discussions with them beforehand about the conditions under which they would wish to live were an inoculation against the guilt that might have followed.

Regrets? Yes, I have many regrets. But in my particular case and in my particular family they are regrets about what didn't happen rather than about what did. There wasn't unconditional acceptance. There wasn't the warmth and closeness I would have wished. There wasn't the giving I had hoped for. But on my part, there was the trying. And I believe there can be satisfaction in trying even when success is lacking.

My anger has mellowed. It's hard to keep blowing on cooling embers. For years before they died, I was angry with two people grown irascible with age, often frustrated with each other, unhappy with the pain of their illnesses, unable and often unwilling to enjoy opportunities that presented themselves. They were who they were, and they waged heroic battles with the aging process. It was hard for me to accept this, because their unhappiness tinted my own life. I wish I could have separated enough to allow them to be angry without that angering me. But I was too invested in "fixing" their pain to recognize that some things can't be fixed and can only be lived through.

The loss aches less now, but contrary to my fears, I have not forgotten much about my parents. I can still hear each of their voices. I can smell my mother's perfume and my father's shampoo. I can see their hands as clearly as if they were in front of me this minute. I remember the arch in my mother's eyebrows and the way the hair curled at my father's neck. I see their smiles. I hear their words. I touch the things they left behind and realize now that they will always be with me, the good and the bad. And I can stop being afraid that I will forget them. I hope that, as I have been told by others further into the process than I, the bad memories will fade and the good ones will remain vivid.

My own mortality is much more of an issue with me since I have taken the point and moved into the position of being the generation next to die. Time has a different meaning. Expense of life energy is weighed and valued differently. And living with newly emerging aches and pains has given me an empathy for my parents that I didn't have when they were alive. I am not yet comfortable with thoughts of my own aging and dying. But I don't need to get comfortable as much as I need to get busy enjoying the time that remains.

So I guess it's safe to say that I have survived the dark night of my parents' deaths and am healing. We put medicine on our physical wounds to protect them from infection and heal them. And I hope that as with the body, there will come a time when my spirit has recovered. I've put my spiritual wounds into words, and my writing has been good medicine for me. So has the passage of time.

Conclusion

When I began this journey with my parents, I was unsure of many things: What lay ahead? Would I be strong enough to help them? Would I know enough? Could I learn enough? Did I really love them? Did they love me? How would we end up feeling about each other? How would it affect my life with my family, with my friends, my job? How did I want it to end?

My only compass was my instinct, my gut feeling about what to do. I got scared. I got lost. I got depressed and angry, frustrated and overwhelmed. Joy surfaced at strange moments and in unexpected places: finding the right gift, discovering a solution, celebrating a milestone, honoring a commitment, sharing family and community. And now that I have gotten through this time, I find myself reflecting on what it all meant.

When I began my story by saying that this is a book about life, about feelings, and about love, I didn't realize how much those things are changed by the experience of caring for aging parents who are dying.

Changes in my life

My life changed forever in the process of helping each of my parents have as good a death as was possible. Ours had often been an uncertain relationship because of who we were. But over a long period, I learned to express many difficult feelings to parents who were sometimes unable to respond. And I came to recognize that their love was often communicated in strange and silent ways: when they understood and accepted my need to place boundaries around helping them; when they allowed me to make decisions on their behalf; when they trusted me with their money and their lives. The reassurance I had wished for my entire life came from them slowly as their lives wound down. New doorways of communication opened, especially between my mother and me.

My relationship with my brother also changed as we negotiated the treacherous shoals of this journey together. Neither united nor at war, there was inconsistency in our relationship as we danced around each other's feelings, trying to share responsibilities. In many ways, as we were slowly saying good-bye to our parents, we were coming to understand parts of each other that we had never recognized. And finally, in the intensive care unit of the hospital, where our parents lay dying, we found common ground in common purpose and came to a comforting relationship with each other.

The quality of time changed for me as my parents' needs devoured enormous amounts of the time I wanted to spend on other things: my family, my friends, my career, maintaining my own physical and mental health. Important priorities were put on hold in order to help them. And as I prepared for and dealt with their deaths, I also had to accept that I had already lived more life than I had left.

Changes in my feelings

As my parents aged and died, my feelings about them became much more intense. Anger was hotter; rage was stronger; love was more poignant and compelling. All my normal emotions were magnified by their illnesses, and often I fought hard for control and balance as my feelings overwhelmed me in times of crisis. And all the time, my goal was to steer a course toward a good closure for all of us. To do this, I had to understand and acknowledge what I was feeling. And often, in order to recognize what I was feeling, I had to ask for help. For me there is no sense of weakness or failure in seeking the advice of a counselor, family member, or close friend. On the contrary, I found another pair of eyes offered me a clearer vision. Most helpful were insights from people who had already completed the journey I was making, because the pervasive feeling of helping my parents die was one of absolute loneliness.

With the journey now behind us, I can see that my parents and I changed many of our lifelong habits of communication and revised many of our misconceptions about one another. Thankfully, it was a mutual process, and as the end approached I felt comfortable with what we had said to each other. I hope my parents felt the same way. And I also hope that had we not been able to speak our hearts to each other, there would have been solace for me in the fact that I had tried.

Changes in My Love

I began this journey hoping I really loved my parents enough to help them through this. I end the journey knowing that I did. And between the beginning and the end came the growth we experienced with each other. As my parents' lives were running out, our love changed remarkably. For us, death was a very clarifying catalyst.

When they began to get ill we had come to a resting place in our relationship. I had come to the understanding that they loved me to the extent that they were capable. It was not enough, but I loved them as well—within the confines of my disappointment. We had separate and unsatisfying emotional lives in relation to each other. Dependence changed that.

As my parents grew frail, our expectations of each other changed. A new protectiveness crept into my love for them. It was mirrored by a new appreciation on their part when they saw me trying to help them. We began to talk more openly about death and we began to say good-bye. Our love became more tangible. I loved them enough to accompany them on this journey; they loved me enough to participate in the planning. Slowly we were moving toward each other.

This dialogue with my parents ended when they died, but my feelings continue to evolve. I understand new things about the love between a parent and a grown child: that self-love precedes other-love; that every child wants to love a parent even when that may be difficult; that withdrawing life support can be an act of love; that in the end, trying to love can be as important as succeeding.

In the past four years I have asked many questions and discovered many things about myself—that I can bear pain, that I can find joy amid sadness, that I can grow in my sensitivities and abilities. I have new perspectives about the continuum of human life and family life, and I see my place along that line more clearly. This book has been my experience. Yours will certainly be different. It may be easier or it may be more difficult. When our parents die we live through the challenge often unaware that we grown children keep the company of each other. It's good to talk.

The loss of a parent is a universal journey that most living souls on earth will make. My parents made it. Now I have made it. My children will make it, and their children after them. We move through endless cycles of days, seasons, and experiences with an understanding that certain things will occur. Afternoon will be followed by evening. Night will come and after it dawn and morning. Spring will herald summer to be followed by fall and winter. Life will end in death.

Just as each time of life has its own kind of love, so too each passage to death has its own kind of pain. Pain is the messenger; growth is the message. It is the conduit to understanding and, finally, to the acceptance of the seasons of our lives. In the words of Kahlil Gibran:

Your pain is the breaking of the shell that encloses your understanding. Even as the stone of the fruit must break, that its heart may stand in the sun, so must you know pain. And could you keep your heart in wonder at the daily miracles of your life, your pain would not seem less wondrous than your joy. And you would accept the seasons of your heart, even as you have always accepted the seasons that pass over your fields. And you would watch with serenity through the winters of your grief.

—*THE PROPHET*